POWER YOUR PATH
TO EXTRAORDINARY SUCCESS

UNLOCK
INNER
GENIUS

CATHERINE MATTISKE

SEPARATE

ONLINE PROFILE QUIZ & TOOLS

AVAILABLE FOR THIS TITLE.

Please visit the website for details:

www.innergeniusnow.com

ALSO BY CATHERINE MATTISKE

Train for Results

Training Activities that Work

Leading Virtual Teams

LEARNING SHORT-TAKE SERIES:

Adult Learning Principles 1

Adult Learning Principles 2

Adult Learning Principles 3

Confident Facilitation Skills

Creative Business Thinking

Customer Service Excellence

Debrief and Feedback Strategies

Effective Time Management

Fast-track Instructional Design

Influencing for Opportunity

Internal Performance Consulting

Leading the Training Team

Listen and Be Listened To

Making Meetings Work

Managing for Performance

Managing Organizational Change

Negotiating for Success

Negotiating for Success - The Next Step

Negotiating the Million Dollar Deal

Persuasive Presentation Skills

Recruiting for Results

Sales Force Leadership

Successful Project Management

The Effective Leader

Understanding and Managing Diversity

Understanding Customer Motivation

Understanding Relationship Selling

TPC - The Performance Company Pty Ltd
Level 20,
Darling Park
Tower 2, 201 Sussex Street,
Sydney NSW 2000 Australia
ACN 077 455 273
email: tpc@tpc.net.au
Website: www.tpc.net.au

National Library of Australia
Cataloguing-in-Publication data

Mattiske, C
Copyright © 2021 By Catherine Mattiske

Unlock Inner Genius: Power Your Path to Extraordinary Success
ISBN 978-1-921547-70-6
Hardcover Version
1. Self Help. 2. Business. I. Title.
Dewey class no: 658.4022
Printed in USA
Distributed by TPC - The Performance Company - www.tpc.net.au

For further information, contact TPC - The Performance Company, Sydney Australia phone +61 9555 1953 or TPC - The Performance Company, California on +1 818-227-5052, or email info@tpc.net.au

Further information on the author can be found at www.id9intelligentdesign.com

ABOUT THE AUTHOR

CATHERINE MATTISKE
CEO AND FOUNDER
TPC - THE PERFORMANCE COMPANY

Australia

Catherine Mattiske is a leading training professional, author, and publisher with an internationally acclaimed career spanning 30 years across various industries, including banking, insurance, pharmaceutical, biotechnology, and retail.

Mattiske established 'The Performance Company,' a leading-edge training and consulting organization, in 1994. The Performance Company has offices in Sydney, Los Angeles, New York, London, and Switzerland.

Catherine Mattiske has earned a reputation for helping clients achieve their personal and business goals across Australia, the USA, United Kingdom, Europe, Africa, New Zealand, and Asia.

Mattiske's client list has a global reach, including high-profile Fortune 100 and 500 companies.

Catherine Mattiske is an accomplished author and publisher. 'Train for Results' (Allen and Unwin) is on academic reading lists worldwide. In 2014, she authored '*Training Activities that Work*' with a group of her Certified ID9 Professionals. Catherine Mattiske released the 27 part 'Learning Short-takes®' series of books. She wrote '*Leading Virtual Teams* In response to

the coronavirus pandemic, an instant best-seller.

Recognized globally for her achievements in business, Catherine Mattiske was a member of the US Congressional Business Advisory Council. Mattiske has been awarded for her influence on US business and was nominated on several occasions for the prestigious Australian Business Woman of the Year.

Since expanding her Australian business to the US and Europe in 2001, Catherine has worked with her team remotely and built a global virtual organization.

Catherine has created or worked on the learning strategies of the largest global organizations. In addition, she has taught many of the world's leading brands to increase their abilities in learning and development.

Catherine has written this book and shares the wisdom of her 30+ years career. In '*Unlock Inner Genius*,' she aims to help people from all walks of life learn and connect with others more effectively.

ACKNOWLEDGMENTS

On hearing the news that I was writing another book, my lifelong friend, Shirley, asked, "how many more will you write?" to which I responded, "when I've run out of things to share!" So, here is book number 31.

But weirdly, this feels much like my very first book. It's the first time I've written to who I refer to as 'the everyone audience.' Whether you're a teenager finding your way in the world, a parent, a business professional, a coach, an entrepreneur, or a grandparent simply wondering how to communicate with your grandchildren better - thank you for being here. I hope you and others around you benefit and find a new way of learning and sharing.

To the thousands of people I have trained, you have been an integral member of my global learning science laboratory. For over thirty years, I've been privileged to watch people learn and communicate. I've wondered why some people learn faster than others and how some can comprehend better. I've observed others who have learning blocks shutting down their learning ability. This book is a culmination of teaching all of you. Your experiences will indeed benefit others who are experiencing similar situations as they Unlock their Inner Genius.

Thanks to the TPC team, who helped me so much. Special thanks and gratitude to everyone who worked behind the scenes to make the book, the online profile, and the Inner Genius supplementary tools and products a reality.

Thank you to my husband and family, who provided me with endless encouragement throughout my writing process.

Specifically, I would like to recognize and thank all who have reviewed *Unlock Inner Genius* for their time and generosity.

To everyone involved, your collaboration and contribution are invaluable.

Thank you!

Catherine Mattiske

PRAISE FOR INNER GENIUS

"Major disruption requires ingenious responses. Catherine leads us in the pursuit of stretching ourselves and team members to full potential to deliver maximum impact. In my experience, people often move to comfort zones in times of crisis and uncertainty. And yet, at these times, we need to draw out people's strengths to take risks, drive team dynamics and deliver outcomes. Unlock your inner genius with this book that helps you unlearn, re-learn and discover what you are capable of and what your team members can accomplish with your leadership."

The Right Honourable Sally Capp
The Lord Mayor of Melbourne
Australia

"Rethinking, relearning, collaboration, and communication have become essential skills for career success in the 21st Century. Timely, the book **"Unlock Inner Genius: Power Your Path to Extraordinary Success"** offers a science-backed roadmap and programmatic guide on accelerating learning agility and communication efficacy. With mastery of **12 Inner Genius Archetypes,** you unlock your own and others' unique learning preferences and strengths; and build trust-based relationships with people different from you through effective communications."

Donald Fan, Senior Director,
Global Office of Culture, Diversity, Equity & Inclusion
Walmart, USA

"Unlock Inner Genius: WOW! I can't wait to add this to my leadership development reading requirements. "We are all teachers. And we are all learners!" I've been training leaders for decades, and this sums up what all aspiring leaders need to strive to become! Inside this book, you will find a personalized roadmap to success for your career that can then be applied to the rest of your life!! A true all-round personal development tool!"

Paul Holba, MBA, Manager of Organizational Development & Training
AAF International (American Air Filter), USA

"In a world where the volume of information is growing exponentially, understanding the optimal way people learn is essential. As both the father of two young children and a CEO who leads a diverse team, personalising how I communicate to each individual is critical. The Inner Genius has given me a practical model to help me recognise and adapt to the learning styles of others."

Jamie MacDonald, Co-founder,
Storypark, New Zealand

"The Inner Genius archetype model provides all educators (professional or in life) to be equipped with knowledge on how others best learn and how to best communicate with all individuals. By understanding each person's preference, one is able to tap into each individual's strength and provide them the space to flourish - even as they learn!"

Voula Powell, Associate Director, Program Manager,
Global Learning Solutions
Takeda, USA

"Unlocking your inner genius for me means capturing the hearts and minds of those I interact with through any channel. Leaders are encouraged to treat employees as individuals, but how do you maintain an individual focus when addressing the team collectively? This book provides the blueprint for achieving this outcome. It IS possible! Communicating individually but collectively means getting everyone aligned sooner and moving people through change in a more seamless way. This is helpful in both business and personal settings. I'm extremely passionate about people's success (family, friends, employees, customers), and communication is a critical element to building each and every relationship. Thank you, Catherine, for the insight on how to be more effective in reaching people on a personal level!"

Mary Poppen, Chief Customer Officer, Glint at LinkedIn and former Chief Customer Officer at SAP Cloud and SuccessFactors, USA

"Talent hits a target that no one else can hit. Genius hits the target that no one else can see, as the wisdom from Arthur Schopenhauer elucidates.

Catherine Mattiske helps you unlock and unleash such uncommon genius in this thought-provoking work.

As the World's beloved genius Albert Einstein put it elegantly, Everyone is a genius! If we explore our inner psyche and idiosyncrasies, we will find such genius. Through 12 archetypes and brain-storming exercises, this book would help you unravel and nurture your Inner Genius. Whether you are a student, life-long learner, educator, or an accomplished professional, this masterfully written book is for you. I highly recommend this book for everyone."

Dr. Mohan K. Bavirisetty, Chief Scientist and Technology Leader, Cisco, USA.

"In 1988, Arie de Gues wrote that, "The ability to learn faster than your competitors may be the only sustainable competitive advantage," and today (33 years later), the pace of change is accelerating at exponential rates. This is certainly true for CEOs but applies to everyone who wishes to succeed in a world that is undergoing unprecedented transformation. Catherine Mattiske developed Inner Genius to provide the tools to understand how we like to learn and how to learn faster. More importantly, she provides guidance for how we can help our organizations, students, and families to also learn faster."

Paul Witkay, Founder & CEO
Alliance of Chief Executives, USA

"Unlock Inner Genius is similar to other personality and leadership style assessments in that it provides individuals with some key insights into how we show up with others. The Genius Archetypes are insightful, and you'll find yourself nodding and thinking about whether your spouse is a "Valedictorian" or your boss is a "Futurist." But while other assessments are heavier on the self-awareness analysis, Genius leans hard into how you use that information to connect better with those around you. As I read the section on "How to Hook in All Archetypes," I found myself furiously scribbling notes on writing an email or creating a presentation that appeals to all learners. It made me want to go back and reframe every important presentation I've given, a message I've sent, or social media post I've created. This book is a complete and practical blueprint for self-awareness of who we are and using that knowledge to connect with others in how they want to be reached. In an increasingly virtual world where everyone is looking for ways to form authentic relationships with others, this book helps us tap into the human in all of us with appreciation and celebration for how our differences make us stronger. "

Jessica Ridlen, Strategy & Operations,
Director - Healthcare Market, Genentech, USA

"I have never believed the saying there is no I in team, there are many inner geniuses in teams. To get individuals and teams humming they need to know their own and other's inner genius. Catherine brings this to life in simple, readable, and understandable ways. If you care about yourself and others, read this book and start to use your inner genius and search for it in others."

Toby Hall, Group CEO
St. Vincent's Health Australia, Australia

"We are living in an era that is branded for unprecedented accelerating disruptions in personal, work, and social life. In order to be successful and resilient in the face of such disruptions, we need to interact with a large diverse set of people, in a positive and productive manner. One of the important ways to tap that interaction and remain empowered is to understand Inner Genius of the self and the Inner Genius Archetype of the people around you. Catherine has provided an absolutely simple, yet powerful framework to tap into Inner Genius that will enable success on an ongoing basis, in all walks of life, that one chose to follow."

Dr. Satyam Priyadarshy, Founder
ReIgnite Strategy, USA.

"As a training professional in industry, and a parent and grandparent, I believe Catherine Mattiske's book, Unlock Inner Genius, should be the book you purchase and read today! Everyone has their own unique Inner Genius. The real power is released when you unlock your Inner Genius and learn to flex to others and their Inner Genius. The result is communication that is more proficient and effective in business and personal relationships. Buy Catherine's book, Unlock Inner Genius, and see how it's done!"

Steve Monroe, Ph.D., Regional Training Director, Nor Pac Region, Airgas an Air Liquide Company, USA

BRAIN FUEL **PROCESSING POWER** **POWER UP**

*Inner Genius is a tool to identify your preference for taking in new information ("**Brain Fuel Profile**").*

*Next, it discovers your choice for processing information ("**Processing Power**").*

*Finally, the process connects your personal ignition tool ("**Power Up Profile**").*

The combination of the three profiles will provide you with your **Inner Genius Archetype**.

CONTENTS

INTRODUCTION

Welcome to the world of Inner Genius!

In many ways, this book seeks to accomplish several things at once. First, it aims to give individuals the tools and information they need to find success in a rapidly changing business and technological climate. And it provides a roadmap for a new way of learning and communicating with the world around us.

Regardless of the career path, industry, or objectives you each have, the world is changing, and so is the way we process information. This book will show you, among other things, how to unlock your learning ability, learn faster, and gain new knowledge easier – all things needed to survive and thrive in this fast-paced, evolving world.

Much ink has been spilled about learning. It is a topic that attracts educators, academic theorists, psychologists, sociologists, philosophers, and more. This is because, very likely, it is an area that influences just about every facet of individual and socialized existence.

Simply stated, learning is one of the most fundamental things we do as human beings. We are dependent on it at a biological level. Without the capacity to learn, we would not maintain our status as the apex biological creatures inhabiting Earth.

The processes by which we accomplish this great activity have been the subject of academic and philosophical debate since the dawn of humanity. For example, what is the most efficient way to achieve learning? When do we introduce critical, specific informational building blocks to those we wish to teach? Should everyone get the same knowledge?

The answers to these questions are paramount to anyone interested in realizing the potential of their human existence. This book will consider some of the ways we can effectively and efficiently re-learn how we learn and elevate our capacity to gather, process, and retain new information. This is no small task.

At one point or another, we have each already been taught how to learn. "Do your homework." That is one I am sure you have all heard. "Read it and highlight the important parts." There is another one. Here, we will explore how well strategies like those work, and if so, they will continue to work in the future for you.

Traditionally learning has been viewed as a singular activity. Someone teaches. Someone learns. We are all learning every day in today's modern world, sometimes from a formal lesson but most often informally.

The term 'teaching' has also traditionally been thought of as conducting a class, training session, or workshop. So, of course, for teachers, educators, and learning professionals reading this, you've educated yourself on the art and science of teaching.

But what if you have not pursued a career in education? You may not instantly consider yourself a teacher. However, we are *all* teachers. And we are *all* learners. As a co-worker, you show others how to work a new piece of technology, complete a form, set up a new meeting type, and more. As sports coaches, managers, or leaders, you guide individuals and groups to attain more skills and knowledge to reach goals. As parents, you teach your child or children every day. Whenever you are imparting knowledge, you want someone to take action in a teaching/learning situation. We simply don't refer to it that way!

TWO ANGLES: LEARNING AND COMMUNICATION

In this book, you'll explore how you can **function optimally as a learner** and **revolutionize your communication skills** to get others to take action. This is not a book on teaching.

Instead, it's about unlocking the genius inside you and how you can communicate in a way that discovers the genius potential of others.

1 - UNLOCK YOUR LEARNING PREFERENCE

You'll **discover your learning preference**: the way that you learn best. *This is how you navigate the world around you.* In doing so, you'll find that you learn uniquely. With this knowledge, the realization hits – if you learn uniquely, that means everyone around you learns differently from you!

2 - UNLOCK SUPERCHARGED COMMUNICATION

The flipside of this book is **communication**. *This is how you interact with the world around you.*

This book answers the questions: How can you communicate and influence people who learn differently from you? How can you share a single message that hooks in everyone, regardless of how they like to learn?

This is the ultimate power of Unlocking Inner Genius. Every email, report, presentation, and conversation may change from this day forward!

Furthermore, in our modern world, the ways information is transmitted and applied are changing. To take full advantage of this new reality, **we must evolve the way we communicate.** But before we can move forward with the complexities of re-learning how to learn and restructuring our communication language, we must first go over some essential elements of the mind and the body.

3

NAVIGATING INNER GENIUS

Here's a sneak peek at what's coming up on the following pages:

- **Part 1** uncovers the power of Inner Genius and who it helps

- **Part 2** explores how we learn and how this has changed over millions of years

- **Part 3** gives an overview of why we have learning preferences

- **Part 4** is where you meet your Inner Genius and explore how your brain takes in, then processes and powers new information

- **Part 5** provides a quick reference for each of the 12 Inner Genius Archetypes

- **Part 6** reveals the tips and tactics to take you to the next level of your *Inner Genius* so that you can customize messages with every Archetype

- **Part 7** is like reaching the summit of a mountain. It will show you how to reach every different Inner Genius Archetype via one communication in one message.

- From the summit of the mountain, you look beyond to see a valley of new opportunity. **Part 8** discusses how you can up your retention of further information through brain storage techniques.

- **Part 9** supercharges your communication by deep-diving into the world of influencing others for a more significant edge.

4

- **Part 10** gives you a template to put your Inner Genius into action, and in **Part 11**, we wrap up Inner Genius!

Yes, learning is mysterious. Communication is the force field that binds us together. It is amazing. There are patterns to the process, and once you find the keys to unlock those on the way you personally learn, you can bring those patterns to life. But, going beyond this is the real advantage. Learning how to unlock the learning of others and communicate in a more advanced way....we'll see that's where all the fun begins!

PART 1.
THE POWER
OF INNER
GENIUS

WHY INNER GENIUS?

WHAT IS INNER GENIUS?

*Inner Genius is a tool to identify your preference for taking in new information (**"Brain Fuel Profile"**).*

*Next, it discovers your choice for processing information (**"Processing Power"**).*

*Finally, the process connects your personal ignition tool (**"Power Up Profile"**).*

*The combination of the three profiles will provide you with your **Inner Genius Archetype**.*

WHY INNER GENIUS?

Until now, the act of learning is mainly self-taught. Rarely are we taught *how to learn*, yet we spend much of our lives in school or learning environments. Every day, we learn from other people or by using Google or informal methods. This is a mystery that is confounding. Why are we taught to learn new *things* but not how to *learn* effectively? We are taught reading, writing, arithmetic, science, and an endless number of subjects. But not learning. Good learners are a product of luck or timing rather than a concerted effort to be taught how to learn.

8

THE BENEFITS OF KNOWING YOUR INNER GENIUS

Knowing your personal Inner Genius Archetype is your unique combination of Brain Fuel, Processing Power, and Power-Up. It is like revealing a new language, often for the first time in your life.

HOW TO BECOME AN INNER GENIUS INTERPRETER

Do you remember the exact day you realized that your native language, your mother tongue, was not the only language, and other people spoke different languages? Probably not. If we could go back to that day and listen to another dialect for the first time, it would undoubtedly be confusing and confronting.

Regardless of which language you learn as a child, the realization that other people speak different languages comes at an early age. For me, I have always spoken English. However, I remember going to school with a girl whose family originated from Germany. I remember listening to my young friend confidently switch between German and English. As I tried to communicate with her mother, she translated my English into German and back again. Thus, even at a young age, she could bridge the gap in communication between her mother and me because she knew both languages.

This bi-lingual or multi-lingual ability is akin to Inner Genius. Think of your learning preference as your learning language. For the first time in your life, this book may reveal that your learning language is different from your friends, family, children, boss, and co-workers. Perhaps your *Inner Genius Archetype* is different from everyone else's around you. And until now, you didn't know it. And, because of this, you may have been challenged to explain things, repeating yourself to make your instructions or points clear, or have become frustrated with other people that 'they are just not getting it.'

There are many unique *Inner Genius Archetypes*, and through the online tool, you'll discover yours. If you haven't found your Inner Genius, you can do so now at:

www.innergeniusnow.com

COMMUNICATING ACROSS ARCHETYPES: IN 'THEIR WAY.'

Once you have discovered your Inner Genius Archetype, you've unlocked your learning language. However, the real power of Inner Genius is learning that there are other Inner Genius Archetypes, all of whom learn and communicate differently. Therefore, to effectively communicate with each different Inner Genius Archetype, it's beneficial to discover their 'language.'

INTRODUCING THE INNER GENIUS ARCHETYPES

A UNIVERSAL LANGUAGE OF LEARNING AND COMMUNICATION

For a moment, imagine that you speak Spanish. But, your 11 co-workers, family members, or friends each speak a different language: Mandarin, Hindi, Arabic, Bengali, Russian, Portuguese, Indonesian, English, Japanese, Polish, and French. But, none of them speak Spanish, like you! Okay, so some of the words are similar in your Spanish language to other languages, that's good; you might be able to get by. And, you learn as you go to speak parts of different languages so that you can communicate. Perhaps you might even find an interpreter. However, it would be very frustrating and exhausting. But, imagine if you could talk in all 12 languages. How amazing would that be? Then, you could effortlessly pick up the language that people speak and talk back to them in 'their language.'

That's just what Inner Genius is about. You have your personal Inner Genius Archetype.

So somehow, communicating with different people with different Inner Genius Archetypes needs to be bridged.

LEARNING PREFERENCE ALGORITHM

The real power comes when you can spot another person's Inner Genius profile and communicate in a way that makes it easy for them to understand you. Then, you'll learn to speak 11 different learning languages and effortlessly switch between each, depending on who you are communicating with.

In this book, you'll learn the algorithm and know how to build this **'translation bridge.'** This applies to spoken communication and also written communication. When speaking to people with a different Inner Genius profile than your own, you are making it effortless for them and for you.

WHO IS INNER GENIUS FOR?

You might be a small business owner, a corporate high flyer, a mother of three, a single dad, a sports coach, a teacher, educator, manager, or a team member. But, regardless of your profession, background, upbringing, or where you are from, we are united by two things:

We all learn new things,
And we all communicate.

These two dimensions of human behavior: **learning** and **communication,** are the foundation stones for unlocking your Inner Genius. This chapter shows a selection of different groups of people where Inner Genius can be valuable. Included is the 'why' for each of these groups:

- **Inner Genius in Business**, specifically for individual employees, for teams, for entrepreneurs, leaders, and managers, for salespeople, for presenters, and for learning and development professionals

- Inner Genius for Educators and Teachers

- Inner Genius for Parents or Parent Figures, and Families

- Inner Genius for Gen-Z, Friends, Co-workers, Roommates, and Partners

- Inner Genius for Students in School or College

- Inner Genius for Sporting Coaches and Community Groups

- Inner Genius for Mentors

However, there is an endless number of people, professions, and groups that will benefit from unlocking Inner Genius for themselves and those around them. So, use the following not as a definitive list but as a guide.

INNER GENIUS IN BUSINESS

Is there a benefit to a company if individual employees and their management teams know their own unique *Inner Genius Archetype?*

Can you confidently build *translation bridges* to other people's *Inner Genius Archetypes,* whether they are co-workers, customers, or managers?

Can knowing these things help me grow my potential and succeed in business?

The answer is yes, yes, and yes! And more...

FOR INDIVIDUAL EMPLOYEES AND TEAM MEMBERS

Let's start with an individual employee. If you are working for a company, large or small, that's you!

BENEFITS FOR YOU WHEN LEARNING

Knowing the preferred way that you take in information, your *Brain Fuel,* and how you process that information, your *Processing Power,* gives you confidence when learning and communicating at work. One of life's most important lessons is how to learn effectively. But even more significant than that is the power of exceptional communication skills.

From day one at a new job, learning is in play as you begin to informally learn from your new co-workers. More formal education occurs as you get signed up for a suite of onboarding courses and essential learning programs provided for all new employees. This might take place as face-to-face classroom learning, online digital learning, or reading. Throughout the entire time, you are an employee, there is always new learning. Whether formal or informal, there's always something new, changing, or some reason to grow. This is the work fuel for lifelong learning.

However, learning can be stressful as you build on what you already know, diving into the unknown to learn and retain new information. If you've ever come out of a training program mentally exhausted, then you've experienced how difficult learning can be. If you can unlock your *Inner Genius*, learning becomes quicker, easier, and less demanding. You'll know your personal learning preferences. Regardless of how the information is coming to you or at you, you'll be able to translate it into your unique method of retaining that knowledge.

Finally, unlocking your Inner Genius will help your existing learning strategies. By providing you with many methods to learn 'your way' and process new information, you'll activate your individual *Inner Genius Archetype* like a pro!

BENEFITS FOR YOU, WHEN WORKING WITH OTHERS

If you've ever been part of a workgroup, meeting, or team where people are saying things or writing documents in a way that simply doesn't make sense to you, you're not alone.

Perhaps you've been talking to a customer. You can't get your message across effectively, leaving the customer frustrated and disgruntled. It's easy to say, 'it's my fault...I didn't understand the customer,' and that may be true, or not! Or, could it be that those people had no idea how to communicate to you in a way that makes sense for your *Inner Genius Archetype*? Perhaps it's not your fault after all. Let's solve this!

When a customer, co-worker, presenter, or boss is talking, or you're reading an email or message from them, they're communicating 'their way.' Whether they happen to know their *Inner Genius Archetype* or not, you'll be in the power position. Regardless of how they communicate with you, you'll be able to instantly translate that from 'their way' to 'your way.' Without saying anything! You'll understand quicker, be able to respond more confidently, and not have to ask so many times for clarification. Pretty good, hey?

BENEFITS FOR THOSE AROUND YOU

You can't change the world, but you can change yourself! It would be a wonderful world if every human knew their Inner Genius Archetype. It would undoubtedly reduce communication blunders and streamline how people converse, write and share.

But, people who know their own Inner Genius Archetype can practice how to spot the Inner Genius Archetype of others. And, when they do, they have a considerable advantage. When people communicate with you, you'll have the *Inner Genius* tools and techniques to interpret their communication – this is a massive benefit to you. Also, while you are communicating, via listening, you'll pick up *their* Archetype and communicate to them 'their way.' So when you are speaking, presenting, or writing to others, you'll be able to flex to their preference – almost like magic!

Daily, when communicating with your teammates and co-workers, managers, leadership, or customers, your Inner Genius radar is in the swing. You'll be searching for the hidden signals other people use to communicate that will give you hints on what their unique Inner Genius Archetype might be.

Once you pick up these hints, you'll be able to flex to their preference. And, you'll be able to communicate with them in 'their way.' Speaking and writing to others in their Inner Genius profile will help you build a *translation bridge* between how you communicate naturally. You'll be able to pivot how you communicate into their preference. This will

15

make communication quicker, easier, and more straightforward.

FOR TEAMS

Imagine being part of a team or leading a group where people's communication was frictionless. Daily interactions were not impeded by misunderstanding, misinterpretation, arguments, ill-feeling, tension effecting downturns in productivity and low morale? What if there was a frictionless pathway for teams to travel in every interaction. Having each team member Unlock their Inner Genius is the first step to being on that pathway.

A NEW TEAM LANGUAGE

In a world where teams are under more scrutiny to meet their team goals, blitz KPIs and are expected to do more with less, team cohesion has never been more critical.

However, in team meetings, some team members feel foolish when they ask why a new initiative is taking place or how decisions impact other people. Others are scared to deep dive into the detail, fearing that they'll look like a progress blocker. Some team members are impatient and want to immediately begin building a solution even before the direction is set. Others glaze over during long presentations of slides filled with numbers and data. At the same time, others are quick to criticize ideas and come up with alternatives, even before the first option is tried. And some are quiet or silent. This is hard to wrangle for team leaders and even harder for team members who often leave meetings frustrated and sighing at the lack of team harmony.

Let's solve this!

Communication is one of the critical factors that contribute to team productivity. Effective communication begins with understanding how each team member learns, takes in new information, processes it, and shares it. When each team member has unlocked their *Inner Genius*, they understand how *they* learn and show up as part of the team. When the whole team knows *each other's* Inner Genius Archetype, a new pathway of communication opens.

Firstly, team collaboration will improve because people know each other's strengths and prefer to learn and communicate. There is no doubt that a variety of Inner Genius Archetypes will be present in one team. And that's a great thing! Each team member recognizes team members who are different from them, which means they know each other's Inner Genius Archetype profile. As a result, they can build a **'translation bridge'** to flex their communication style to the other person's Inner Genius Archetype during everyday work. Then, the team can get the job done quicker and more effectively.

Inner Genius provides a new team language. The team will naturally communicate in a new way. Instead of glaring at the person who asks 'why' all of the time, they'll appreciate that that individual needs to know this before they can be fully effective. They'll appreciate the detailed person and understand that it's their dotting every 'I' and crossing every 't' that is a valuable asset. And, for the people quick to build and change the rules, they'll be aware and be able to slow them down where necessary and let them play, explore, iterate and invent when it's needed.

In an Inner Genius fueled team, you'll hear people say things like:

- "Okay, it's over to you, Ama; you are our Mason. How can you start constructing this? What do you need to get started?"

- "Shelby, you're a Futurist. What do you see as some new ideas that we haven't thought of?'

- "Adesh, you're our Horologist. Can you put together a work plan so that we can get building next week?"

- "Shanice, as our Narrator, who do you think you need to meet with to explain why we're doing this new initiative?"

Everyone has their unique Inner Genius Archetype. The real power is when you unlock yours and know everyone else's profile. Then, individuals can communicate with each other in the other team member's preferred way. Once the team begins to use each other's individual strengths and talk in each other's Inner Genius language, the team inertia will ignite. Team goals – blitzed!

STEPS TO UNLOCK YOUR TEAM'S INNER GENIUS

A fun and insightful exercise for each team member is to unlock their *Inner Genius Archetype* using the online *Inner Genius* profile tool. First, allow time for each individual to read and reflect on their unique Inner Genius Archetype. You'll probably find that sharing each's other profile amongst team members happens naturally. However, there is an opportunity for harnessing the potential of the team's *collective Inner Genius*. We suggest that the results are openly shared at a special team meeting devoted to Inner Genius. You'll find resources and tools on the Inner Genius platform to assist team leaders or a nominated team member in facilitating the discussion.

Each team member must realize that they all bring strengths to the team and that how they individually learn and communicate is an asset to the team. No one should ever feel ostracized or pigeon-holed because of their profile. Unlocking Inner Genius never puts people in a 'box' or a 'type.'

Sharing each other's profiles moves the conversation along to discover the possibilities of how the team as a whole can maximize their learning and communication effectiveness. In addition, providing opportunities for a team member to practice new communication methods and converse differently will transfer their learning to action.

At their next team meeting, we suggest regrouping as a team with two main agenda items. Firstly, a reflection on how unlocking their own Inner Genius has helped them and the team. And, secondly, to discuss how the team will use their collective Inner Genius to flex their communication outside of their team. Discussions could center around communicating cross-functionally with other teams, leadership, and external groups like external partners and customers and how to maximize that success.

Team members are genuinely intrigued and excited when they harness their collective Inner Genius. Communication becomes frictionless, and their engagement skyrockets.

FOR ENTREPRENEURS, SENIOR LEADERS, AND MANAGERS

In the past, much has been written about different leadership styles and approaches that can help leaders be more effective. By understanding how and why they do what they do and assisting leaders in identifying where and when they need to adapt their style, leaders can increase their effectiveness and confidence.

Every leader, manager, and entrepreneur has different decision-making styles and ways of working. They also have different methods of synthesizing information and learning. Some need to observe. Others need to be in the trenches with teams doing the work. And some leaders need regular updates via highly visual reports. In contrast, others are pleased to receive information verbally through phone calls or meetings.

As explained in this chapter, it's most likely that senior leaders have individual employees with unique and different learning preferences. Having discovered that each employee has a unique *Inner Genius Archetype* is genuinely eye-opening for leaders. Realizing that all employees have individual profiles, unique ways of learning, methods of synthesizing and processing new information, and a multitude of communication preferences can be an amazing revelation.

Where does this leave leaders who are driving the business vision?

With so many variants within teams, how can a leader communicate in a one-size-fits-all message?

How can they lead their organization's success and growth when followers are potentially not speaking the same learning language?

In daily interactions, how can leaders adapt their style to reach each Inner Genius Archetype?

How can leaders, managers, and entrepreneurs quickly spot different preferences and adapt their communication on the fly?

Let's dig into some solutions...

THE POTENTIAL BENEFIT OF BONDING LEADERSHIP WITH LEARNING PREFERENCES

Peter Mirski and Reinhard Bernsteiner in 'Relationship between Learning Styles and Leadership Styles: A New Perspective to Encourage Learning in the Workplace,' discovered four components of transformational leadership that can be identified when learning preferences are taken into account:

1. **Individualized consideration**: support of followers by providing learning opportunities; individual needs are recognized and respected.

2. **Intellectual stimulation**: intellect and creative ways of thinking are appreciated; the willingness to change is encouraged

3. **Inspirational motivation**: a vision and an optimistic view towards the future is communicated; confidence that all goals can be achieved and that goal achievement changes the future positively is demonstrated

4. **Idealized influence**: leaders are seen as models who are respected and admired; they enjoy the confidence of their followers

The findings also point out that, to create a positive atmosphere and stimulate motivation for learning in the workplace, leaders must apply leadership styles according to the needs of the employees. If they experience their preferred leadership style, the employees can exert their innovation potential.

DISCOVERING INNER GENIUS FOR LEADERS

The first step of building a *translation bridge* to 'hook in' different learning and communication preferences is to first understand your own profile.

There are many unique *Inner Genius Archetypes*, and through the online tool, you'll discover yours. If you haven't found your Inner Genius, you can do so now at:

www.innergeniusnow.com

PUTTING INNER GENIUS INTO LEADERSHIP PRACTICE

'Adapting your leadership style' is a throw-away phrase that is definitely easier said than done. Consciously thinking about how you communicate and potentially changing it every time you write an email, speak or present, participate in meetings, create documents for company-wide distribution, or meet with people externally may sound like a burden, not worth the effort. Initially, as you unlock your own Inner Genius and then take steps to unlock other people's true potential will be a conscious effort.

This conscious effort is actually called learning! There are four levels of competence:

4 - UNCONSCIOUS COMPETENCE

3 - CONSCIOUS COMPETENCE

2 - CONSCIOUS INCOMPETENCE

1 - UNCONSCIOUS INCOMPETENCE

Unconscious Incompetence is when people 'don't know what they don't know.' As a result, they are unaware that there is an opportunity for improvement or a problem to be solved. For example, think about when you were a teenager considering getting your driver's license. Even though you'd been a passenger in a car for your whole life, your parents knew that you 'didn't know what you didn't know' about driving a car. You might have been like me thinking, 'how hard can it be?'

And then you got in the car and attempted to drive. Immediately you were catapulted from Unconscious Incompetence to **Conscious Incompetence**. "I know that I don't know how to drive a car." You immediately knew that you didn't know. And it hurt! Suddenly, the road became a giant pathway of fear, and the car was controlled by a dazzling array of pedals and switches. Even though you'd been in a car all of your life, driving was new.

Then, driving became more manageable with every practice session and driving lesson. "I drive very carefully" With heightened concentration driving on city streets and with a coach or teacher by your side. This is the stage of **Conscious Competence**.

Now driving is probably second nature. Reaching **Unconscious Competence** is when you can drive without thinking about pedals and levers, at the same time listen to music and your navigation system, and effortlessly chat to passengers as you get to your destination.

Embracing Inner Genius will have the same 4-Levels of Competence, much like driving a car.

The following describes a possible learning journey for leaders and managers as they move through the levels:

1 - Unconscious Incompetence. At this point, you are unaware of the Inner Genius profiling tool and its potential advantages it may have for you as leaders, learners, and communicators.

2 - Conscious Incompetence. Awareness of the Inner Genius tool happens, and people might be talking about their Inner Genius Archetype. You hear of groups embracing a new way of working within their teams. Perhaps you think that having everyone unlock their Inner Genius will be a valuable initiative for your organization. As a leader, manager, or entrepreneur, you are now aware of the advantages. Still, you don't know your personal Inner Genius Archetype, how to use it for yourself or your employees.

3 - Conscious Competence. You discover your Inner Genius Archetype and study the attributes of your unique profile. You then begin to communicate with other people differently. Next, you try to spot their preferred way of learning through heightened awareness of what they are saying and how they say it. Finally, you pivot your language in written and spoken communication, building *translation bridges* to communicate in a way that everyone prefers, not just you. It's a concentrated effort.

4 - Unconscious Competence. You now structure written and spoken communication differently. Every email that you write, presentation, report, and conversation is balanced for all learning preferences. Your direct reports are responding quicker and more highly engaged. You've noticed that the number of clarifying questions has reduced. When people communicate with you, you can expertly translate their style into your preferred style and pick up new information quicker. You've now started using your powerful communication style with friends and family, and it's working. And, with your new understanding of how you prefer to learn best, you seem to be able to get through new information faster without feeling overloaded.

I'M FINE! AN OPPORTUNITY LOST

Not adapting your leadership style to be more balanced in your communication style is a lost opportunity. Every person is unique, and you are potentially making it unnecessarily more difficult for those with whom you are communicating when there is a more advanced method at hand.

Not making an effort to understand these nuances can lead to frustrations for you and your direct reports and other employees. In extreme circumstances, when a leader's personal Inner Genius Archetype is the polar opposite of an employee, they feel little connection between them and you. By understanding how employees learn, their learning preferences, and communicating to them in 'their way,' leaders can assign managers and teams the most appropriate tasks in line with their strengths and convey information in a way that is most likely to resonate.

FOR SALESPEOPLE

Learning how people learn is a hidden secret shared amongst elite salespeople. Great salespeople don't give the same proposal, pitch, or presentation to every customer. Customizing their messaging to tap into how their customer prefers to learn new information and communicating in the customer's preferred style raises the bar well beyond traditional selling.

Selling to customers with different Inner Genius Archetypes is a shift in written and spoken communication.

Some customers will respond to glossy brochures or presentations filled with charts, stunning photographs, and handouts. Ensuring that your presentation slides are professional, filled with color, charts, graphs, and pictures are essential for these customers. In addition, after a sales presentation, providing professional materials and supplementary documents will help these customers embed what you've presented and have materials for future reference.

Other customer types will be more receptive to the salesperson talking through their proposal, articulating the features and benefits, concepts, and project plans. For them, PowerPoint or Google Slides are not all that helpful. Instead, they'll hang on to every word that you say and repeat back what they've heard for clarification. Therefore, it would be best to limit written correspondence with this customer type and summarize long emails and reports to succinct bullet points backed up with facts and figures.

Compared to the other two groups, you might encounter other customer groups that are anxious to meet, perhaps over a drink or coffee, and may take more of a 'gut feel' approach to working with you on a project, initiative or purchase decision. Engaging this type of customer is essential by 'showing' not 'telling.' Getting them involved, walking through project plans, or purchase options will boost your effectiveness. And, in turn, boost your sales results!

So, as a salesperson, how do you know which sales strategy is best?

- How can you pivot your presentation and pitches to best meet the customer's preferred way of learning?

- How does this work in a busy retail shop or online store when dealing with so many customers in quick interactions?

- When presenting to a group of customers, how can one salesperson meet the preferences of the entire group?

The questions are endless and probably require a book all of its own. There's an idea! But, for now, let's look at some quick wins.

FIRST, KNOW THYSELF!

I'm assuming that you've been reading this entire chapter. In that case, you'll know that step one is to first understand how you learn, process, synthesize and store new information. Once you uncover this, you might reflect on the types of your existing customers you're naturally drawn to and communicate with the best. Chances are, they might be a similar Inner Genius Archetype to you. Likewise, we are naturally drawn to people who learn like us because we speak, essentially, the same learning language.

There are many unique *Inner Genius Archetypes*, and through the online tool, you'll discover yours. If you haven't discovered your Inner Genius, you can do so now at:

www.innergeniusnow.com

A NEW PATHWAY OPENS

If you think that once you know your own Inner Genius Archetype, the pathway to success will appear miraculously before you. Then, you're a little correct, but a lot 'not quite yet.' Unfortunately, there's no genie in a bottle and no three wishes! Sorry!

Knowing how you learn is a tremendous bonus because you'll translate in whatever form the new information is coming to you and build a *translation bridge* to your preferred learning method. That will make learning easier, faster, and less stressful. For example, imagine your next sales conference. If you are the type of person who finds it challenging to sit and listen to marketing presentations, sales leader presentations (even when you know that you should be focused), you're not alone. When you unlock your Inner Genius Archetype, you'll be better equipped to focus, absorb, and synthesize the presentations, ready to take action.

The pathway to personal success will undoubtedly open because you'll be learning quicker and more effectively. But let's think through the actual end game.

The end game for salespeople is to achieve or exceed sales goals.

FOR PRESENTERS, TRAINERS, EDUCATORS, AND TEACHERS

Professional teachers, learning and development professionals, and educators know that a single teaching approach doesn't work for every learner.

TRANSFORM LEARNING LESSONS TO BECOME BALANCED

When unlocking a learner's Inner Genius, the key for teachers and trainers is to learn to flex and pivot to ensure that all Inner Genius Archetypes are being met.

This may sound impossible, but with practice, you'll be transforming learning lessons into balanced workshops filled with interest for all learners. Accolades will flood in for you and managers, participants, parents, and others, to acknowledge you for your ability to hook into every learner, regardless of their learning preference.

The better you understand how people learn, the better you can teach. It sounds so fundamental, but you'll be able to precisely deliver what learners need and how they need it. You'll be able to approach teaching more akin to a facilitator, coach, or mentor, rather than someone who is there to sprout their knowledge. By grabbing your learners' attention and increasing engagement, you'll enhance their understanding of new knowledge, accelerate their learning speed, maximize learning transfer, and motivate every learner to apply what they are learning. All of this saves time, effort, and money.

In the corporate environment, learning and development leaders refer to creating High Performance Learners who collectively form a High Performance Learning Culture.

In this book, we provide you with the *Inner Genius Wheel*. It's a tool for structuring and delivering every content topic that you train, present, or teach.

FIRST STEP: UNLOCK YOUR INNER GENIUS

First, you'll need to do a deep dive into your own personal learning preference to achieve a heightened outcome. By completing your Inner Genius Archetype profile, you'll understand how you prefer to learn, and importantly where you have to step into the Archetypes of others.

There are many unique *Inner Genius Archetypes*, and through the online tool, you'll discover yours. If you haven't discovered your Inner Genius, you can do so now at:

www.innergeniusnow.com

SHORTCUT: UNLOCK PARTICIPANT'S INNER GENIUS

Once you have discovered your own Inner Genius Archetype, you'll be able to hone your communication skills in readiness for teaching in a balanced way. When you teach or present in a balanced way, you'll be hooking in all participants by communicating and building *translation bridges* to every participant or student.

"But I have a large group of students. How will I be able to quickly learn to spot who's who and then communicate to each Archetype individually?"

It's a fair question. It does take time to re-language a natural way of speaking, especially when you are imparting knowledge and new skills to students or participants.

There is a shortcut that many educators, learning professionals, and teachers take. Have each student or participant complete their own Inner Genius profile.

If you are not in a position for your learners to complete their profile, don't despair. You can do your profile and become aware of the profiles and design for all in a balanced way so that all learning preferences are equally assimilated into every topic and lesson you teach.

The ultimate advantage of communicating in a balanced way is asking your learners to complete their Inner Genius profile. Imagine the power of knowing the combined Inner Genius profile of your class! You'd know who is a Mason, a Catalyst, who has the Archetype of the Cartographer, and more. You'd know who's who!

And, you'll know your own Archetype profile, so that will give you insight into how far you need to personally stretch away from your personal learning preference to meet your group of learners where they are and take them where they need to go.

As a teacher, educator, presenter, or corporate learning professional, this will give you the jump-start before preparing or starting a class, workshop, or course.

For your students or participants, it will help them increase their self-knowledge on how they prefer to learn during your class. And during the course, participants can maximize their potential and reduce their personal learning stress.

HOW DOES KNOWING EVERYONE'S INNER GENIUS PROFILE LOOK IN ACTION?

In addition to knowing their individual Inner Genius Archetype, each participant will learn what strengths they bring to individual and group activities. And you will as well.

Let's look at an example.

Let's say you set a case study activity where small groups have to analyze a case study and suggest a solution.

EXAMPLE – INNER GENIUS *NOT* IN PLAY

Without knowing the individual Inner Genius profiles, you might group your students into small groups, set the activity, give them time to solve the case study, and then perhaps have them share their solution with the whole class.

The flow of the activity might look like this:

- Regroup to groups of 4-6 (randomly)

- In your groups, read the case study

- Discuss the problem and form a solution

- Present your solution to the whole class

EXAMPLE – INNER GENIUS *IS* IN PLAY

Let's flip the switch now to the same activity when you, their teacher or trainer, *know the Inner Genius profile of each participant.*

Firstly, your grouping would be nuanced. The best group mix is a balanced blend of learning preferences that maximizes learning for everyone. Most likely, you'd choose a well-balanced small group in line with their profile. The optimum small group would be a representative from each Brain Fuel profile and each Processing Power Profile.

Next, you'd bump up the intensity of the activity to make it a rich learning activity. In this case study example, you might have a series of questions for the group to work on, and the new activity flow might look something like this:

- Regroup to the assigned groups (tell each person which group they are in)

- In your groups, read the case study

- Collaborate as a group to create a flipchart/use an online tool such as Jamboard/fill out a worksheet to answer these questions:

    1. What is the relevance of the case study to how you work/ your life?

    2. List the elements of the case study that led to the problem

    3. How would you solve the problem, realistically?

    4. If you had all of the resources in the world, would your solution change? What might your answer become? How could you create a game-changer?

- Present your list, realistic solution, and game-changer solution to the whole group

COMPARE THE PAIR

The first is designed for only one Inner Genius Archetype, The Scribe. The second, for all 12 Inner Genius

Archetypes. The second example is beautifully balanced to hook into each learning preference so that everyone feels like the lesson is built for them.

As their teacher or trainer, you have employed a balanced approach to the lesson. Therefore, the pace of learning will increase. That means that participants will be operating faster. So, both examples above will take the same amount of time yet, will have two vastly different outcomes.

PADDLERS OR WADERS?

Take a moment to think of a fast-flowing river with a relatively steep gradient causing an increase in water velocity and turbulence. When navigating the river, it's way easier to shoot the rapid using ingenuity, a safe canoe or kayak, a paddle, and a life jacket. But, on the other hand, it's way harder, perhaps impossible, to wade *up* the rapid, against the river's force trying to get upstream without a canoe or kayak, just yourself.

People's learning journey is like the river rapids. When people learn *with* their learning preference, they are in their canoe or kayak, with their paddle going with the river's flow. It may be challenging at times, but they go with the flow and get down the river safely. When people are learning *against* their learning preference, they may feel like they are trying to get up the river against the force of the water, feeling overwhelmed and exhausted.

As a teacher, educator, or professional trainer, it's essential that **you** make the learning journey (the river) as effortless as possible for your student or participant. By hooking into their learning preference, *building translation bridges* means that everyone will be learning *with their preference*. When this happens, self-confidence, motivation, energy, and ability soar. For you, their teacher, you're their guide, in their canoe or kayak with them every step of the way, safely navigating them through the rapids to the end goal.

And each participant is in a different canoe or kayak (because they have a different learning preference), but that's okay. Because you can flex your style, you're in every boat with them! That's the power of teaching with Inner Genius in play.

UNLOCKING GROUP LEARNING USING INNER GENIUS

Having each participant or student unlock their own Inner Genius is the fastest way to revolutionize a lesson, course, or entire curriculum. Once the speed of learning increases, the depth and understanding of new concepts will grow, and the stress of learning will decline.

Overall, you and your class will be operating at warp learning speed by creating a language of learning.

There are many unique *Inner Genius Archetypes*, and through the online tool, for each of your participants to unlock. To unlock the Inner Genius for every participant, you can do so now at:

www.innergeniusnow.com

INNER GENIUS FOR PARENTS OR PARENT FIGURES, AND FAMILIES

It's easy for parents or parent figures to celebrate when their child gets a good grade or wins a contest. But, what about when children find learning difficult and, despite their perseverance, they just are not "getting it," or they experience success in one subject but struggle with others? Or, what happens when a parent gets frustrated when they have difficulty teaching their child something new, only to give up? Teaching takes time and patience for parents, and often, they resort to saying, 'do your best,' which may not be unlocking the true potential for the child.

We receive our children without any instructions, rule book, or warranties. Yet somehow, parents are supposed to magically add the role of 'teacher' into their world. And help children navigate their education when perhaps they have no prior formal teaching experience. Whether in a traditional classroom setting or homeschooling, it's a parent's duty and privilege to help children learn. But, perhaps for many, it's easier said than done.

Learning happens at home, school, interactions between home and school, and in neighborhoods and communities. Unlocking a solid knowledge and communication connection between formal and informal education will create positive attitudes and set children up for lifelong learning.

Parents are in the 'box seat' to unlock the Inner Genius of their children. Understanding how each child learns and processes differently improves daily communication and fosters a child's strengths and preferences.

Every child learns differently, and importantly, your child may learn entirely different from you, their parent, or parent figure. This is because each of you potentially has a different *Inner Genius Archetype*.

DISCOVER YOUR OWN INNER GENIUS AS A PARENT

Unlocking *your child's* Inner Genius starts with finding the keys to unlock *your* Inner Genius.

Perhaps you are a parent who learns best by seeing new information, drawing, doodling, creating flowcharts, reading, or designing outstanding school event posters. These parents enjoy taking children to the movies, art galleries, supplying their children with arts and crafts materials, reading to their kids, and encouraging reading.

Maybe you are a parent who loves to listen to your favorite music, podcast series, or audiobooks. These parents fill their homes with music, encourage their kids to learn a musical instrument, engage in lively family discussions, or get children reading aloud. In addition, they might encourage children to record what they need to know and then play it back to enhance their learning or enter them in the school spelling bee.

Or, perhaps you are a parent who rarely sits on the couch. Instead, you are someone who is always on the move, loves building new things, likes sports, or loves to paint or do flower arranging, jigsaws, helping with school projects, cooking, or working on the computer. These parents probably purchased building blocks for their young children and practiced hand-clapping when they were infants. As children get older, these parents encourage sport, dance, take family holidays that include lots of activities, like hiking or going to the beach.

The examples here provide an insight into the first step of Unlocking Inner Genius: *Brain Fuel.* That means discovering how people take in new information from the outside world. However, this is only the first part of getting the key to unlock Inner Genius. There are three parts to unlocking your Inner Genius: Brain Fuel, Processing Power, and Power-up. This unique combination, your Inner Genius Archetype, is a powerful tool to forge a successful path for everyday living.

What you love to do daily helps you to understand how *you* learn and communicate with the world. How you learn is reflected in how you communicate as a parent. *Step one of working to unlock Inner Genius is to first discover your own Inner Genius Archetype.*

The power of knowing your own *Inner Genius Archetype* is to also know that your child's profile is likely different from yours. For example, if you live in a two-parent household, both parents potentially learn and communicate differently compared to each child. So, how can you build a **translation bridge** between your preference and theirs?

DISCOVER YOUR CHILD'S INNER GENIUS

One way to determine your child's learning preference is to actively observe them daily. Watching their actions, interests, and daily activities will help parents begin unlocking the mystery of their learning. But, unfortunately, this is slow and may not result in much of an outcome.

To truly understand how you can unlock your child's Inner Genius, you'll need to find out their *Brain Fuel* and then their *Processing Power* and their individual *Power-Up*. The combination of all three forms their unique *Inner Genius Archetype*. And, if you have multiple children, they generally all have their own unique Inner Genius Archetype.

As a parent, once you know each child's Inner Genius Archetype, you can communicate with your child individually, in 'their way.' Reflect on how many times you've asked your child to do something, and they've either not understood or done something completely different. Reflect on how many times you've been trying to help them with homework or teaching them something new only to get glazed eyes or, worse, boredom and total switch off. Reflect on the frustration and perhaps arguments you've both felt during these times.

BUILDING PATHWAYS FOR SUCCESS

As we discussed early, knowing your children's *Inner Genius Archetype* is like unlocking their learning language and, for you and them, a world of new communication possibilities. And instead of you speaking Spanish and them French (in other words, you both communicating in your own *Inner Genius Archetype*), you suddenly know their language and communicate in their way.

So, if you knew this, what would be the impact on your daily life?

- How would siblings interact differently if they knew each other's Inner Genius Archetype?

- What would be the benefit to the household harmony if everyone was communicating at a more advanced level?

- How could this benefit you, the busy parent who juggles work, family, and activities?

- What could be possible in your children's lives if you could help them to unlock their learning and help them create a pathway for unlimited success?

This book will show you that the possibilities are endless, painless, and available. Imagine the power of Inner Genius for your family!

INNER GENIUS FOR GEN-Z, FRIENDS, CO-WORKERS, ROOMMATES, AND PARTNERS

Are you hanging out on Instagram? Tik Tok? Pinterest? YouTube? Perhaps a dating site? Are you a social media influencer or one of the influenced audience?

The internet has evolved to include a robust set of communities where meaningful conversations are happening and different perspectives are shared. Likewise, social media channels have grown from simply sharing photos of food and selfies to being part of a digital toolbox of help as people need it.

All generations use the internet to communicate and learn daily. But, let's hone in on one group, Gen-Z, and discover how they can unlock their Inner Genius. And, if you have friends or family members in Gen-Z, then you'll want to unlock how you communicate with them as well.

The questions to explore include:

- Do Gen-Z learn differently from previous generations?

- How can I effectively teach or communicate with Gen-Z?

- I'm in Gen-Z, yet one of my biggest frustrations is communicating with people in my age group via technology. How can I iron out the creases?

The short answer to 'are they different?' Yes...and...No!

Let's start with some basics and build up from there.

WHAT ARE THE CRITICAL DRIVERS OF GEN-Z?

Gen-Z includes those born between 1997 and 2012. According to USA Today, Helen Wang, an associate communication professor at the University of Buffalo, said, "They grew up immersed in rich media, and they are naturally equipped with better digital media literacy skills to navigate across different platforms competently and nimbly."

According to Pew Research Centre, Gen-Z is unique when compared to the generations before them. Unlike Baby Boomers, Gen X'ers, and Gen Y's, people in Gen-Z are the most diverse generation of our time. Here are some facts:

- Generation Z's attention span is eight seconds. That's how long they need to decide if something is worth their time.

- Be that as it may, 59% of Gen-Z'ers continue their education in college. For comparison, 53% of Millennials enrolled in college.

- Almost a third (30%) of Generation Z members major in science and social sciences. Only about 10% choose "business" as their major.

Not only is Gen-Z the most diverse generation, but it will be the most educated one. Despite their short attention span, Gen-Z'ers manage information better than their predecessors. At least in terms of education, that is.

EXPLORING HOW GEN-Z LEARNS

So, let's think about how this group learns uniquely and how they are driven by peers, their families, friends to pursue their passions and communicate in the world around them.

Learning for Gen-Z is different. For example, 98% of Gen-Z's own a smartphone. In fact, they don't know a world without the internet and smartphones. So it's easy for them to learn new technologies and adapt their thinking. Effectively, they have most of the world's knowledge in their hand – ready for them to learn.

Notably, their world is very different from the experiences of generations before them. Their language has evolved to include new expressions across many new communication channels. However, their **learning preferences** remain largely unaltered.

Moreover, results of scholarly research indicate that these 'digital natives' are influenced by technology. Still, it is not deterministic for how successfully they **learn**, despite claims by the popular press, educators, and organizations selling learning programs.

UNLOCKING THE INNER GENIUS OF GEN-Z

Unlocking the Inner Genius for people in Gen-Z, and those with whom they interact, be it other Gen-Zers or older and younger people, is important and urgent. When compared to previous generations, their world is changed, but the physiology of their brains has not.

How can they navigate their world better?

Effectively Learners are Learners: Gen-Z has more opportunities and the capability to learn via technology. And, at its core, communication remains unchanged. Gen-Z chooses to communicate via technology as effectively as they do in person.

For Gen-Z and everyone interacting with them, optimizing learning and communication between friends, co-workers, roommates, and partners include daily learning and communication.

Maybe you are a Gen-Z and have been part of tricky conversations with friends as you decide where to holiday. Some friends want to go one place, others desire a completely different experience, to the sigh of others.

Or perhaps you've attempted to teach a Gen-Z friend the latest technological device and have become frustrated. Again, it's likely because you don't know the difference between how you learn and how your Gen-Z friend learns. But, again, as we explained before, it's a bit like you speaking one language and them speaking another.

HOW IS IT THAT SOME GEN-Z PEOPLE BECOME INFLUENCERS?

Often, people feel like they are not hooking in the people they are communicating with and not making their point clearly enough.

When online, why do some people influence thousands of followers, yet others don't? With one simple Instagram post, people are hooked in and freely commenting and engaging.

This ability to 'hook' people in can also be face-to-face in serious conversations with friends. But this lack of 'hooking people in' can also happen even during the simple times of chatting with friends. For example, you might be discovering new ways to navigate life or having weird conversations that only become poignant and meaningful after a time of reflection.

Some people have the best ideas in meetings, or collaborative projects yet are overlooked for someone else who claims credit because they could communicate the idea or concept better. Frustratingly, people who get the credit often get promoted, leaving behind the most innovative people. Learning to unlock your Inner Genius in a work situation will help you to stand out in the world.

When dating or in relationships, miscommunication is raging, especially if it's communication happens digitally. Imagine if you could speak the learning and communication language of your date, your roommate, or your prospective partner.

Learning how to unlock your *Inner Genius Archetype* and learning how to communicate with your friends, roommates, dates, or partners own individual *Inner Genius Archetype* is a vehicle for people to speak about themselves to someone else. It's a way to ask for what you need and influence others. It's a way to share learning, teach others, and succeed. From the most minor decisions to the most serious conversations, from the most informal learning opportunities to formal education, knowing how to unlock the Inner Genius for yourself and others is a breakthrough.

INNER GENIUS FOR STUDENTS IN SCHOOL OR COLLEGE

Every student absorbs, processes, and retains information differently. Who taught you to read, write, speak, listen? Probably your parents and teachers. But, who taught you to learn?

As a student, it's never too late to truly understand how you learn. It's paramount to building self-confidence, improving your self-image, and giving you a true reflection of your innate strengths. Knowing your learning preferences may also inspire your creativity and innovation, spark your curiosity for further learning and form a love of lifelong learning.

But how will it benefit you in an academic situation? Unlocking your Inner Genius will give you a head start to maximize your learning potential. It will help you succeed at school, college, or university because you'll have unique techniques for understanding information, regardless of how it's delivered to you. As such, you'll score better on exams, assignments, and tests.

Knowing your Inner Genius Archetype is a considerable boost. You'll be learning 'your way' building the best strategies for yourself. Also, suppose you have a lousy lecturer, poor instructor, or dull teacher. In that case, you'll be able to reduce the stress of learning and apply new study strategies to gain success.

Then, when you leave your studies and enter the professional world, you'll have the edge over your colleagues. Your well-honed learning skills will improve your influence and persuasiveness. When others struggle to create presentations and reports, you'll do it with ease. And, when you are promoted to manage a team, you'll be able to do so effortlessly because you've been practicing communicating and building *translation bridges* for years. In short, you'll transform your learning power into earning power!

INNER GENIUS FOR SPORTING COACHES AND COMMUNITY GROUPS

Sports coaches and instructors help children and adults to realize their potential in a sporting discipline by giving advice, instruction, and encouragement. It's in teaching new skills, tactics, and techniques, plus monitoring and enhancing performance by providing encouragement and constructive feedback where Inner Genius can be a powerful tool. As a coach's primary skill boils down to communication, one of the traps for a coach is to coach how they personally learn.

Each coach will have athletes with various learning preferences that play out during practice sessions and competitions. Let's look at how a coach who knows Inner Genius could cater to these different profiles. A coach may have some athletes or team members who stand back and observe and are careful. For these styles, athletes could watch others, and the coach might create an environment where perfection is not expected on their first try. Other athletes are quick, confident, and get straight to the point. For them, the coach, focused on peak performance, can ensure that their practice session is clearly linked to the game strategy and real-life gameplay. Perhaps a coach has one or more athletes who perform best at practice sessions to fit new skills and facts into coherent approaches. The coach might explain the background, practicalities, nuts, and bolts of what they are about to learn and practice for this group. Finally, coaches may find themselves with team members who are open-minded, enthusiastic, quick to jump in, and want to center the practice sessions around themselves. The coach needs to allow these athletes time to experiment, dive into an activity, and work it out as they go. The coach might then ask reflective questions to think through and discuss after the session or at the next practice session. A well-versed coach in unlocking Inner Genius can cater without fear or favor to the different learning needs of each team member.

> *"Practice doesn't make perfect.*
> *Perfect practice makes perfect."*
>
> Vince Lombardi, American Football

Every athlete learns using their own unique *Brain Fuel* and *Processing Power* preference. And, each athlete potentially posses a different *Power-Up*. That means there are many profile combinations that a coach may have on their one team of athletes. And, most likely, most are different from the coach's personal profile!

Being *unaware* of how each athlete unlocks their own Inner Genius potentially slows down athletes. As a result, they may never reach their potential as they try to learn *against* their learning preference.

For a coach, the first step to unlocking Inner Genius is knowing their personal Inner Genius Archetype. Then, knowing each athlete's Inner Genius Archetype follows. Some athlete's and coaches' profiles will be similar or complementary, sometimes worlds apart. As a result, coaches can build depth in their coaching practice and communicate in a new way. They will have each athlete unlocking their potential and can create personal learning pathways for each individual.

PART 2. LEARN OR LAPSE

Learning is a process that never ends. We cannot help but add knowledge and build a stronger mind as we go about our lives; the least we can do, though, is make sure we are doing this efficiently and effectively! In this section, we will really focus on how we can bolster and improve our learning. Learning can be passive, sure, but it does not have to be! When we take the steps needed to ensure we are operating at our highest level, we can begin to really see some magnificent results.

The reason we call this section "learn or lapse" is simple, those who take a passive approach to learning are going to fall behind those that take a more active approach. If you want to supercharge your learning, you absolutely can—we are certainly going to show you lots of ways you can do that. If you sit back and wait, you are very likely going to lapse.

By looking at precise processes in our minds and in our social settings, we can uncover brilliance. Here, we will explore how these processes impact our day-to-day cognitive operations, our learning, and how all of these things impact and are affected by our biology. So, with that, let's get started!

THE SCIENCE OF LEARNING

In this section, we will step inside the "brain laboratory" and take a look around. Our brain is a fascinating, complex, and mysterious place. Study after study has unlocked new information (and often created new mysteries!) that have helped shape how we view and study the human experience.

One of the most important reasons we study the human brain is because we need it to do, well, everything! Learning is no exception, and without understanding how the brain works, it is nearly impossible to craft efficient and effective learning techniques. Luckily, we have made great strides in this area already.

One question we often find ourselves asking is, "Why is some learning so hard?" Outside of the well-documented clinical deficiencies inhibiting some young learners—think dyslexia, Attention-Deficit/Hyperactivity Disorder, Dyscalculia, etc.—there are still other less-diagnosable reasons learning new information can be challenging.

For an explanation about why some types of learning are so hard, let's take a look at what Psychology Today has to say about the matter.[1]

The journal offers some insight into the challenges we all face when it comes to learning new information. They dive into some possible theories about what might be holding back individuals and posit some ideas about why learning is so complicated sometimes.

---

[1] https://www.psychologytoday.com/us/blog/jacobs-staff/201501/if-learning-is-natural-skill-why-is-it-so-hard

47

One possible explanation cited is relatively blunt. Learning is hard "because we think it is," reads the publication.

"... Because we have been trained to think it is. Because we have been inundated by the fears of people who look back on their lives with regret over lessons they hadn't learned," explains author Po Chi Wu, Ph.D., who at the time the information was published was teaching at the School of Engineering at the Hong Kong University of Science and Technology.

One reason we struggle, he says, is due to one of the most basic human instincts we possess: fear. He said he believes there is an uncomfortable resistance to learning that has taken hold, and it may be self-inflicted.

"Are we as individuals and companies afraid of learning? How did we become this way? What has happened to our natural instincts of curiosity and survival?" asks the author.

You, the enterprising reader of this book, though, are not afraid to grow your mind and expand your thoughts! If you were, you would not be here reading this book. One of the things we are going to do is lay out the groundwork for overcoming all of the challenges and obstacles associated with learning. Then once we have overcome those challenges, we will push deeper into the most cutting-edge approaches to rapid information retention and synthesis.

The conclusion we have reached, and the one we believe you will ultimately reach, is that learning really is not all that difficult at all, so long as you have *both* the right attitude *and* approach. By the time we are done, we are confident you will have everything you need to cultivate both of those elements.

NEURONS THAT FIRE TOGETHER, WIRE TOGETHER

Another important question we need to ask ourselves is, "What exactly is learning?" The question might sound silly on the surface, but in truth, it is actually far more complex than people realize. For example, is learning a process, or is it a result? Is learning permanent?

The answer to these questions may be as much philosophical as they are biological. However, the actual physical process by which new information is received and processed is definitely a critical element to consider in response to the question. To that end, we see that learning definitely has a physical component to it, and so do its processes.

Circling back to Psychology Today, the impact of "curiosity," a natural precursor to learning, is one that is both measurable and definable. Reads the Magazine: "When we exercise curiosity, our brain releases dopamine, a biochemical neurotransmitter. One of the side effects of dopamine is that our brain interprets that as pleasure. The result is a positive feedback loop: Curiosity => dopamine => pleasure => curiosity.

This is excellent news! While we may be inhibited by one natural human instinct—fear—we are also bolstered by one as well: pleasure. According to Po Chi Wu's analysis, the hungrier we are for new data, the happier we will be, quite literally.

Like anything else, the better we become at something, the more likely we are to enjoy that something. To that end, learning has a built-in biological positive feedback loop that will help push us in the right direction. All we have to do is embrace it!

BRAIN BASICS

KEY TERMS FROM THE NATIONAL INSTITUTE OF NEUROLOGICAL DISORDERS AND STROKE[2]

The Central Nervous System is the physical entity that does the heavy lifting when it comes to information processing in our bodies (read: learning). This system is made up of the brain and the spinal cord. There are two basic types of cells in this system. First, there are **neurons**, and second, there is **glia**. Depending on which part of the brain you are looking at, there might be more of one than the other. However, notes the medical resource, neurons are the key players.

"Neurons are information messengers. They use electrical impulses and chemical signals to transmit information between different areas of the brain, and between the brain and the rest of the nervous system," reads information from the institute. "Everything we think and feel and do would be impossible without the work of neurons and their support cells, the glial cells.

Neurons have three primary components: 1) **cell body**, 2) **axon,** and 3) **dendrite**.

"Neurons communicate with each other by sending chemicals, called neurotransmitters, across a tiny space, called a synapse, between the axons and dendrites of adjacent neurons."

This communication is the foundation by which learning is made possible. In fact, without these processes, it would be impossible to "think" in the colloquial way we use the term. Therefore it represents one of the most critical functions we perform.

---

[2] https://www.ninds.nih.gov/Disorders/Patient-Caregiver-Education/Life-and-Death-Neuron

A natural extension of this process is **memory**. As you can imagine, memory plays a crucial role in learning. Strengthening your memory is an integral part of becoming a better learner, so it stands to reason that doctors and researchers have spent a lot of time understanding how it works.

SO, WHAT EXACTLY IS MEMORY?

"Memory is the ongoing process of information retention over time. Because it makes up the very framework through which we make sense of and take action within the present, its importance goes without saying," reads information from The Derek Bok Center for Teaching and Learning at Harvard University.

"In light of current research in cognitive science, the very, very short answer to these questions is that memory operates according to a 'dual-process,' where more unconscious, more routine thought processes (known as "System 1") interact with more conscious, more problem-based thought processes (known as "System 2").[3]

Further, in scientific terms, when we *get* information, it is called **encoding,** and when we hold it, it is called **storage**. Finally, accessing that information is known as **retrieval** or **recall.** According to the teaching center, understanding the relationship between these stages is imperative when making decisions about how to present information.

"With a basic understanding of how these elements of memory work together, teachers can maximize student learning by knowing how much new information to

---

[3] https://bokcenter.harvard.edu/how-memory-works

introduce, when to introduce it, and how to sequence assignments that will both reinforce the retention of facts ... and build toward critical, creative thinking," they say.

LEARNING VS. MEMORY

Learning can be defined formally as the act, process, or experience of gaining knowledge or skills. In contrast, memory can determine the capacity of storing, retrieving, and acting on that knowledge. Learning helps us move from novices to experts and allows us to gain new knowledge and abilities. Learning strengthens the brain by building new pathways and increasing connections that we can rely on when we want to learn more. Definitions that are more complex add words such as comprehension and mastery through experience or study.

THE CAVEMAN, THE SCHOOLMARM, AND THE SEARCH TOOL

The evolution of education is one that, interestingly, looks a little different than the evolution of other concepts, ideas, and practices. While there is no doubt that advancements in education and educational theory have contributed significantly to improvements in efficiency for the transmission of information, some of the most impactful and effective elements of teaching have endured since the dawn of humankind. We will discuss some of these areas in greater detail below, but for now, just keep in mind that education, at its core, will universally carry with it specific characteristics. This is a crucial reality to keep in mind going forward.

Education is, by nature, a social consideration. In this way, we can separate it from "learning," which can be done by anyone, either alone or with others. For example, you can "learn" the names of all United States presidents by studying a list of those names. With that learning, you'll be able to recite or recall them when needed. Education, on the other hand, is a systematic exchange of information done in an institutional setting. Like many other social elements, education is a natural process that has existed in some form or another since human beings evolved into the organisms we see before us today.

A MILLION YEARS OF LEARNING THE TRADITIONAL WAY

To that end, the cavemen and cavewomen that predate us today, by a couple thousand years, also engaged in the education of one another, much like we do now. Human beings, apparently, are hard-wired to share what they know with others. This transmission of information started in the caves and eventually progressed into a more modern iteration involving buildings and campuses. Now, education can take place virtually anywhere, thanks to technological advancements like video chat and powerful search engines like Google. In the coming sections, we will explore this lineage and parse through some of the ways education has changed and some of the ways it has not.

The earliest forms of education that took place were heavily reliant on several elements that we still use today, although not quite the same way as our ancestors. As the evidence suggests, the first humans emphasized storytelling, symbolism, problem-solving, and their environment.

Let's dig deeper into each of these elements.

STORYTELLING

Storytelling is as much a part of the human condition as nearly anything else we do. We use it to connect on emotional, spiritual, professional, and social levels. As a result, we are constantly telling stories, even when we do not realize that we are doing it.

Why do we do this? Because stories are handy ways to transmit ideas. Stories represent our most potent means to give context to the thoughts and ideas that comprise our existence. They create a bond between the teller and the listener that cannot be replicated or recreated in any other way. They are unique and powerful.

Consider this advice from Harvard Business.

"Good stories do more than create a sense of connection. They build familiarity and trust and allow the listener to enter the story where they are, making them more open to learning. Good stories can contain multiple meanings, so they're surprisingly economical in conveying complex ideas in graspable ways. And stories are more engaging than a dry recitation of data points or a discussion of abstract ideas."4

Storytelling, simply stated, is a remarkably effective way to teach and learn. Why? Because stories are easy to remember, notes Harvard.

"Organizational psychologist Peg Neuhauser found that learning which stems from a well-told story is remembered more accurately, and for far longer, than learning derived from facts and figures. Similarly, psychologist Jerome Bruner's research suggests that facts are 20 times more likely to be remembered if they're part of a story."

---

[4] https://www.harvardbusiness.org/what-makes-storytelling-so-effective-for-learning/

SYMBOLS

Interestingly, there is a lot of evidence to suggest that some of the most detailed and involved pieces of cave wall art, which are thought to have been one of the earliest forms of idea transmission known to us, may have actually been much more nuanced than initially imagined.

Researchers cited in The Guardian found that in many instances of wall art, a series of seemingly disparate and abbreviated-looking symbols were actually just an emerging form of note-taking meant to transmit more significant ideas in a short-handed way. In other words, the basics of language were being formulated one little picture at a time.[5]

Reads The Guardian:

> "For the symbols provide clear evidence of the way our ancestors moved from representing ideas realistically – as in those beautiful images of bison and mammoths – to the stage where they began to represent concepts symbolically. In some cases, signs appear to emerge from the use of truncated images of an animal and eventually come to act as a symbol for that animal in its entirety. For example, a wavy line used to depict the back of a horse in a larger painting eventually comes to stand for the entire horse in different sets of paintings."

---

[5] https://www.theguardian.com/science/2012/mar/11/cave-painting-symbols-language-evolution

These symbols' importance and their usefulness as the basis of language cannot be overstated. These symbols were the basis for the story-telling techniques that came to represent the original pedagogical strategy that has defined education for millennia.

Even the most simple designs were helpful to the cave people who drew them. The connection between more complex images and their symbolic representations was all that mattered; so long as the shapes meant something to the viewer, they were helpful.

"There are triangles, squares, full circles, semicircles, open angles, crosses, and groups of dots. Others are more complex: drawings of hands with distorted fingers (known as negative hands); rows of parallel lines (called finger flutings); diagrams of branch-like symbols known as *penniforms*, or little sketches of hut-like entities called *tectiforms*," notes the Guardian.

All of them were useful in one way or another. All of them meant something to the very first educators and their students.

This symbol-based transmission of ideas and vital information—understanding their surroundings literally meant the difference between life and death for the cavepeople—represented one of the most powerful learning tools and techniques ever conceived. Yet, curiously, the contemporary educational theory has moved away from this story-driven approach and, instead, more toward fact-based information exchanges.

ENVIRONMENT

Similarly, another way humans have the capacity to learn is through interaction, manipulation, and immersion with our environment. Our environment occupies a massive chunk of our consciousness, and its impact on us is both active and passive. Simply stated, we must come to terms with our environment, understand how it impacts us and learn to deftly navigate through it day-to-day.

So, what sorts of things compromise our environment? Indeed, a big part of our environment is where we live. But, of course, so too are surrounding dwellings, natural features, friends and family, neighbors, and even strangers co-inhabiting the areas we spend time in. Thus, our environment is complex, multi-faceted, and dynamic. In these ways, it provides an excellent venue to learn.

Interacting with our environment allows us to obtain first-hand information by experiencing that information. Thus, we are learning not because we are being *told* something but because we have *experienced* something.

This is the type of learning that is irreplaceable. Leveraging our environment is a significant part of our natural learning processes. But, unfortunately, it is also one that does not get enough attention in modern educational systems.

Human beings have a long history of interactive, environmental learning. It is the base concept supporting educational initiatives like apprenticeships, training, military exercise, and more. These transmission methods rely heavily on being present, absorbing ambient data, and learning through submersion. Conceptually, environmental learning will always be a part of the human experience. This reality has far-reaching impacts on our entire existence.

INGENIOUS PROBLEM SOLVERS

As a result of the intimate relationship and understanding with our environment, humans are particularly adept at solving problems from that environment. Some might even say that we are "ingenious" when it comes to solving these problems.

What makes us such adept problem solvers, and how can we tap into that reservoir of innate ability more easily? Well, there are several essential things to note concerning our ability to overcome obstacles. For one, human beings have a remarkable capacity for creativity. That creativity must be practiced and nurtured.

Another way we achieve problem-solving is through the use of tools. Fittingly, the development of these tools is often the result of our inherent creativity. The World Economic Forum explains precisely how this works in practice.[6]

According to research conducted at the Massachusetts Institute of Technology's Center for Brains, Minds, and Machines, humans rely on three "critical capabilities" to solve problems that manifest in physical form. These include having prior knowledge of a related situation, an ability to imagine and visualize the impact of our actions, and a capacity to rapidly update strategy when they fail."

"Human beings are naturally creative tool users. When we need to drive in a nail but don't have a hammer, we easily realize that we can use a heavy, flat object like a rock in its place. When our table is shaky, we quickly find that we can put a stack of paper under the table leg to stabilize it," reads information from the research. "But while these actions seem so natural to us, they are believed to be a hallmark of great intelligence — only a few other species use objects in novel ways to solve their problems, and none can do so as flexibly as people."

---

[6] https://www.weforum.org/agenda/2020/11/human-behaviour-problem-solving-skills/

We must cultivate our problem-solving abilities and strengthen them through them with practice. Super-charged learning relies heavily on mental gymnastics and exercise. Overcoming complex challenges is one of the best ways that we can accomplish this, and it is critically important that we do so at every opportunity.

THE TRADITIONAL CLASSROOM - WHAT HAS CHANGED AND WHAT HAS NOT

Change can be difficult. We are naturally inclined to feel safe doing what we know, and we take comfort in the familiar. Classroom teaching has, of course, evolved a great deal in recent years. Education, after all, is one of the most rigorously studied areas in all of academia. However, many of the elements of classroom teaching have, for better or worse, remained intact.

The "Traditional Classroom," so to speak, has many identifiable characteristics that we can point to when studying the effectiveness of that classroom.[7]

"Traditional teaching is concerned with the teacher being the controller of the learning environment. Thus, power and responsibility are held by the teacher. They play the role of the instructor (in the form of lectures) and decision-maker (in regards to [curriculum] content and specific outcomes)," reads information from Innovative Teaching Methods and Strategies.

In this setting, teachers believe that students have "knowledge holes" filled with new information. Conceptually, this theory holds that the teacher, then, is the

---

[7] https://innovativeteachingmethods.wordpress.com/about/traditional-teaching-methods/

primary driver of the learning and, as such, has a more active role than the student.

Learning in this environment, say the Innovative Teaching Methods Strategies blog, is often competitive.

"The lesson's content and delivery are considered most important, and students master knowledge through drill and practice (such as rote learning). Content need not be learned in context," it adds.

There are, for many in the education profession, some extremely valid criticisms of this model. Often, when a teaching model focuses on the teacher rather than the student, the environment becomes rigid and regimented. For example, traditionally, teachers were encouraged to talk "at" their students rather than "to" or "with" their students. As a result, concepts like collaboration are lost.

Much of this type of learning has been replaced by more updated models that leverage the incredible power that technology and innovation have made possible. Further, many of the shortcomings of this model have been exposed by both research and innovative practices that refocus the learning model on the learner rather than the teacher. Depending on who you ask, where you are, or what age learner you are dealing with, you will find varying degrees of the old elements and the new elements in teaching and learning strategies.

One thing you have probably heard time and again as a young learner is "sit still and listen." This was the mantra of the grade school teachers of yesteryear. For a long time, there was a belief that you could shoehorn information into the minds of both younger and more mature learners by simply talking the information into their brains. As we came to learn, this is not the most effective way to teach most learners. At the time it was conceived, it was simply the most prominent theory around.

However, we have come a long way in the education field, and we are no longer reliant on such static methods to exchange information. "Sit still and listen" had its place. But we are in a new age of learning now. We are now ...

LEARNING IN THE DIGITAL AGE

Without taking too much time going over the remarkable processes that led to the digital age we live in, it is worth noting that in the history of civilization, never have technological advancements concerning information exchanging and gathering comes on so fast and become so widespread.

With few exceptions, quite literally, anyone can learn just about anything they could possibly want to know with little in their way. No, we understand the caveats associated with the financial considerations regarding access to this data. Unfortunately, not everyone on the planet has a laptop with access to Google. We are certainly sensitive to this fact. Economics aside, the *potential* for someone to learn at will has never been more tremendous, and the realization of that reality is happening exponentially thanks to the efforts of both public and private entities.

GlobalFocus offers some helpful insights into understanding how we got to this point and where we can go from here. In truth, we are on the cusp of an age in which the very nature of information exchange has progressed to virtual instantaneousness. Yet, too often, the power of that reality is lost on us as we muddle about our days.

"We live in the information age (aka the digital age), which is a period in human history characterized by a shift from industrial production to information and computerization, changing significantly how people interact with businesses and each other," reads information from the Magazine.[8]

The benefits of living in this age extend far into every aspect of social life. Teaching and learning are fundamental pieces of childhood development, but they are also essential pieces of human development. As children, we learn as a way to ensure survival and growth once we move past the caregiver stage. As adults, knowledge and learning extend to socially and politically relevant considerations. For this reason, new and innovative learning strategies are especially necessary.

"Today, information is readily available and free. The democratization of access to information has resulted in a shift in the distribution of power between government and citizen, retailer and consumer, manager and employee, teacher and student. Today, there is too much information for any one person to handle, and that information becomes obsolete very quickly. Continuous, just-in-time access to the latest information has become paramount for all actors in society," reads information from GlobalFocus. "In this new era, being really good at learning how to do new things results in a competitive advantage."

The magnitude of this shift cannot be overstated. It is vital for global citizens to have access to the most up-to-date data and apply that data practically. One of the first steps we must take to unlock our potential as learners are acknowledging the sheer magnitude of what is available to use; then, we must leverage it.

One of the things we hope to accomplish in this book, as we mentioned earlier, is showing students (young and older alike) a better way to learn. The aim, essentially, is meta-learning. Previously, students were taught things like language and math, which was the end of their educational journey; no one ever really taught anyone *how* to learn.

---

[8] https://www.globalfocusmagazine.com/digital-age-learning-2/

This relatively new concept is critical when we talk about super-charging our learning experience. Before we can begin to fully embrace the digital age, we must be shown how to navigate in it. We have to *learn* how to navigate it.

Luckily, to help accomplish this, says GlobalFocus, we have the benefit of being "hyper-connected with analytics everywhere." In the digital age that we live in, it is imperative that learning is done collectively and benefitting the myriad paths of communication available to us.

The new focus on learning is to do it as a socialized member of the information elite. Once learning was seen as a primarily individualized activity, it is now seen as something much more collaborative.

"Digital age learners must be able to connect with learning resources, information, peers, and experts to effectively learn in the digital age. Providing simple tools that enable these connections is important for learning organizations," says Global Focus. "Additionally, analytics can provide insights on the learners, their own development needs, what assets can meet their needs, how those assets are consumed, how learning can be improved, and how effective learning activities are."

There are lots of benefits to this new collaborative approach to learning. However, outside of the synergistic benefits, the rapid pace at which information is exchanged, and the apparent ability to seek and exchange specific data bits, there is an inherent benefit to collaborative learning that does not get enough attention: emotional security.

As discussed earlier, there is a lingering fear of learning that pervades many younger and older students. The possibilities of what we can know are endless, and that can be overwhelming. Yet, when we learn together, we build off each other's knowledge bases and provide an anchor for one another as we continue to explore the vastness of the digital universe we live in.

CORPORATE TRAINING AND ON-THE-JOB LEARNING

One area, in particular, we see this new team-oriented learning model unfurl is in the corporate setting. In business/corporate training, learning takes place for two primary reasons. The first is the ensure that employees have the basic skills necessary to do the work being asked of them. This usually entails learning internal protocols and procedures, workflow habits, organization cultural norms, and tasks specifically related to the day-to-day work expected of a new employee. Again, this could be done individually or in a team setting.

Additionally, the second tier of learning comes after this preliminary exercise. This is the type of professional development aimed at learning what to do and how to do it at a high level. This experience is usually highly collaborative and often includes industry-wide participation, such as the type you might find at a regional or national conference. There, you are likely to see the full measure of current technological capacity on display, as well as face-to-face information exchanges, presentations, and demonstrations of the most cutting-edge research available in your respective space.

LIFELONG LEARNING

Remarkably, people can learn from the moment of birth. However, learning can and should be a **lifelong process**. Learning shouldn't be defined by what happened early in life or only at school. We constantly make sense of our experiences and consistently search for meaning. In essence, we continue to learn.

In today's business environment, finding better ways to learn will propel organizations forward. Strong minds fuel strong organizations. We must capitalize on our natural styles and then build systems to satisfy needs. Only through an individual learning process can we re-create our environments and ourselves.

THE IMPACT FOR YOU

What does this all mean for you? It means a whole load of good stuff, actually. We are now immersed in a sea of new educational approaches rooted in technology, the science of the brain, and, as you will see in a little bit, remarkable advancements in the ways learning can be tailored to the individual learner.

We no longer live like the cave folk, and our ability to exchange information is no longer limited to immediate geography. You do not even need to go to an actual "school" if you really did not want to. Learning has never been more accessible than it is right now. Super-charged learning, as it stands, is entirely up to you. These are inspiring times! Let's not waste them!

SUMMARY

- The earliest forms of education that took place were heavily reliant on several elements that we still use today, although not quite the same way as our ancestors. As the evidence suggests, the first humans emphasized storytelling, symbolism, problem-solving, and their environment.

- We must cultivate our problem-solving abilities and strengthen them through them with practice. Super-charged learning relies heavily on mental gymnastics and exercise. Overcoming complex challenges is one of the best ways to accomplish this. It is critically important that we do so at every opportunity.

- Change can be difficult. We are naturally inclined to feel safe doing what we know, and we take comfort in the familiar. Classroom teaching has, of course, evolved a great deal in recent years. Education, after all, is one of the most rigorously studied areas in all of academia. However, many of the elements of classroom teaching have, for better or worse, remained intact.

- In the history of civilization, never have technological advancements concerning information exchanging and gathering come on so fast and become so widespread.

- With few exceptions, quite literally, anyone can learn just about anything they could possibly want to know with little in their way. Economics aside, the *potential* for someone to learn at will has never been more tremendous, and the realization of that reality is happening exponentially thanks to the efforts of both public and private entities.

- In business/corporate training, learning takes place for two primary reasons. The first is to ensure that employees have the necessary skills to do the work they are asked for. Additionally, the second tier of learning comes after this preliminary exercise. This is the type of professional development aimed at learning what to do and how to do it at a high level.

PART 3.
HOW DO
YOU PREFER
TO LEARN?

This next section will explore more deeply the specific processes and strategies required to maximize the speed we learn. In other words, we will look at ways that we can "super-charge our inner genius," so to speak. However, to do this, there are a few essential steps we must first take.

1. One, we have to identify **how we learn most effectively**, and

2. Two, we must also learn (see, there is that learning how to learn again!) **how to efficiently process new data** so that we do not waste time and energy during the learning process.

To accomplish this, it is beneficial to understand what "type" of learning profile we have.

Not everyone learns in exactly the same way. Identifying the operative elements impacting a learner and which style of learning best suits that learner will help them more efficiently absorb and process new information.

"Learning profiles can be used to differentiate topics, method of learning, and manner of demonstrating learning in a classroom. A student's learning profile is the complete picture of their learning preferences, strengths, and challenges and is shaped by the categories of learning style, intelligence preference, culture, and gender," reads information from EL Education.[9]

Inherently, each person has different characteristics that influence their ability to learn. The above-stated categories says Carol Ann Tomlinson, an expert in educational differentiation, are essential considerations instructors, and teachers need to consider as they prepare lessons for their students. No matter what stage in the learning process you might be in, these factors will tug, push and pull your educational experience. The most gifted instructors will know precisely how to identify a student's profile and play to their strengths.

Says Tomlinson: "There are many ways to accommodate students' preferred ways of learning. Looking for good learning fit for students means, at least in part, trying to

---

[9] https://eleducation.org/resources/helping-all-learners-learning-profile

understand how individuals learn and responding appropriately."

While these differences are essential to know and understand as you consider your own learning preference, it is also important to remember that each learner is unique. There are billions of people on this planet, and none of them are precisely the same. Learning is highly nuanced, and generalizations are not finite rules. If something works for you, lean into it.

Further, just because learners might benefit more or less from one type of learning tactic than another does not mean that each one does not have some merit on its own. For example, some ideas are better transmitted visually rather than auditorily regardless of the type of learner benefitting from the information.

It can also be helpful to practice learning via transmission styles that are not intuitive. For example, if you are a hands-on learner, try strengthening your visual learning skills or vice versa. In some cases, you may not have a say in how the information will be transmitted to you, so it is helpful to bolster your other skills for the instances where you might not be able to learn in the style of your preference.

Ideally, you will be able to translate incoming messages to your preference in most cases. Of course, it may not be practical or even beneficial for this translation to occur with *all* data transmission. If possible, try to pull incoming information using the learning style you are most comfortable with within most instances. In other words, take advantage of what you are good at, but leave a little room to practice a bit of everything else as well.

So what should we do with this information about learning styles and profiles? What is the goal? Ultimately, we want to "super-charge" your learning experience and extract the inner genius inside of each of you. It is there! We just need to unlock it.

TURBO YOUR LEARNING

ATTENTION, RETENTION, MOTIVATION, AND APPLICATION

At the end of the day, all of this information is being presented in order to lay the groundwork for our broader goal of increasing the speed and effectiveness in which one learns. How can we speed up the information retention process and boost the amount of data one can process?

One strategy we can use is "observational learning," as it is described in Britannica. This strategy hinges on the idea that modeling one's behavior after other individuals with the desired information and traits will ultimately lead to learning those behaviors and information rather than simply mimicking them. This includes modeling attitudes, emotional expressions, and behaviors note Britannica.[10]

Over my 30-year career in professional learning and development, I have created a straightforward model that summarizes many behavioral theories. Four steps can be used to accomplish this modeling. They are **attention, retention, reproduction,** and **motivation**. So let's take a closer look at those four steps here.

ATTENTION

"If an organism is going to learn anything from a model, they must be **paying attention** to it and the behavior it exhibits. However, many conditions can affect the

---

[10] https://www.britannica.com/science/observational-learning

observer's attention. For instance, if the observer is sleepy, ill, or distracted, he or she will be less likely to learn the modeled behavior and imitate it at a later date," reads information from Britannica.

This stands to reason. When engaging in this strategy, be confident that you have done all you can to give yourself an edge. Like anything else we do as human beings, learning is done most efficiently when we take care of our most basic biological needs properly. As we noted before, there is a great deal of biology impacting our learning ability. Be sure to get enough rest, eat well and try to get a proper amount of exercise. If we want our minds working at total capacity, we must support them by taking care of our bodies, too.

RETENTION

Next, you will need to **remember** what you saw. This requires focus. Not everyone has the same capacity for retention, so this stage may require more work for some than others. This is OK. Most importantly, do your best at each stage of modeling; the more effective you are at each one, the more they will compound and build off one another.

MOTIVATION

This is a big one. Learning is not going to happen by accident. It needs to be done affirmatively and **with intent**. In this way, the learner must be **adequately motivated** to continue to engage in the steps mentioned above.

"If the human or animal does not have a reason for imitating the behavior, then no amount of attention, retention, or reproduction will overcome the lack of motivation," reads the information from Britannica. "... several motivating factors for **imitation** ... include knowing that the model was previously reinforced for the behavior, being offered an incentive to perform, or observing the model receiving a reinforcement for the behavior."

Together, these four steps represent a natural way to quickly learn a new skill. Unfortunately, in many instances, we go through these stages without even realizing we are doing them. This is especially true of younger learners. However, if we can **actively engage them** during each of the overall stages of our educational journey—be it young, developing, or advanced—we can rapidly build our knowledge base.

APPLICATION

At this stage, the learner is **essentially practicing the behavior** witnessed and memorized over and over again. This requires visualization and physical action, and it incorporates several different elements of learning all at once. In time, practicing and applying a given behavior will not only achieve its execution but an understanding of it outright. This is the ultimate outcome of learning.

*Without application, it is fair to say
that no learning has taken place.*

Francis Bacon's phrase, "Knowledge is Power," written in 1597 and used during the 1800s by Thomas Jefferson in his letters, is a misnomer still quoted today by businesspeople and academics alike.

*In truth, 'knowledge is power, but
only if **put to use**. "*

In other words, unless you apply what you've learned, putting it into practice in a use case, then knowledge is pretty worthless.

A NOTE ON INFORMATION OVERLOAD

As we progress through this book, we will discuss many ways that information can be picked up, synthesized, stored, and applied. One of those methods was just discussed. First, however, it is crucial to remember that we must be aware of certain traps that we might fall into as we progress as learners.

One such trap is "information overload." More or less, problems are the combination of knowing that there is virtually unlimited data available and then simultaneously trying to learn it all at once. In this way, we can get quite "tangled," so to speak. So, how can we untangle ourselves from this information overload and avoid some of these traps and pitfalls?

For one, we must first be *aware* of the problem before we can *address* the issue. Even for the most super-charged learners, it is possible to go too fast and too hard sometimes. Simply acknowledging this now can go a long way in ensuring that your educational journey is not needlessly encumbered.

The temptation to try to learn everything all at once can be daunting. With each new skill or data set, we learn we immediately crave more. Recall back to the immense pleasure we can derive from itching our curiosity. This can become addictive. We risk, though, by pushing too hard is burnout; burnout is never good no matter what context we are talking about it.

You might be able to identify the early stages of problems related to information overload by simply taking regular self-audits. Is your attention waning? Are you having trouble with retention? Is there regular sleep and rest taking place? Ask yourself these questions often and pay attention to any changes in these areas. Like anything else, if you do not foster and facilitate a healthy mix of progress and respite, you will not be able to achieve your best results.

THE IMPACT FOR YOU

You are likely engaging in observational learning all the time without even realizing it. This is especially true of things we have an authentic interest in. We cannot help but engage in the four steps mentioned above when it comes to these areas. Suppose we could take this reality a step further and start more aggressively engaging in this type of learning during the course of our normal, day-to-day routines and activities. In that case, we can give ourselves a tremendous edge when it comes to supercharging our learning.

There are so many significant advantages to absorbing information through observation— none more remarkable than the fact that the opportunities to learn by observing others are virtually endless. There is always something new that we can learn given the proper circumstances. The trick is to create those circumstances as much as possible. This will generate mountains of further information for us to tap into.

SUMMARY

- Observational learning hinges on the idea that modeling one's behavior after other individuals with the desired information and traits will ultimately lead to learning those behaviors and information rather than simply mimicking them.

- This includes modeling attitudes, emotional expressions, and behaviors.

- Four steps can be used to accomplish this modeling. They are attention, retention, reproduction, and motivation. Let's take a closer look at those four steps here.

- o **Attention** - For you to learn from a model, you must pay attention to the model and its behaviors.

- o **Retention** - You will need to remember what you saw; this requires focus.

- o **Motivation** - Learning will not happen by accident; it needs to be done affirmatively and with intent.

- o **Application** - The learner (i.e., you) must practice the behavior witnessed and memorized repeatedly. This requires visualization and physical action.

- It is crucial to remember that we must be aware of certain traps that we might fall into as we progress as learners.

- One such trap is "information overload." More or less, problems are the combination of knowing that there is virtually unlimited data available and then simultaneously trying to learn it all at once.

- Even for the most super-charged learners, it is possible to go too fast and too hard sometimes. Simply acknowledging this now can go a long way in ensuring that your educational journey is not needlessly encumbered.

PART 4.
MEET YOUR
INNER
GENIUS

FUEL, PROCESS, & POWER-UP: A THREE-STEP PROCESS

Here, we are going to examine a super-charged learning strategy.

This one comprises a process that has a greater emphasis on the biological functions associated with data processing.

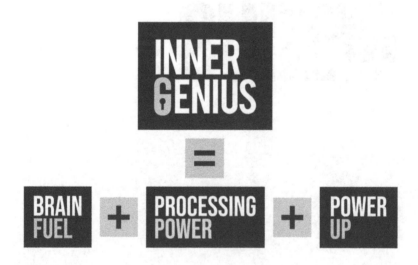

In practicality, using the fuel, process, and power-up method primarily starts simply being aware of how it works and then consciously nurturing its individual elements. Then, our aim is to be more cognizant of how it works and incorporate it into our day-to-day activities.

Ultimately, this learning strategy boils down to identifying your preference for taking in new information, which is your "*Brain Fuel*," and then figuring out your preference for processing that new information. This is what we call your "*Processing Power*." This creates your Inner Genius Archetype. Then, we add onto your Inner Genius Archetype your unique *PowerUp*. This is like a fuel shot that makes you, you!

The first step is to understand how you input new information into your mind. That's your '*Brain Fuel.*' After that, we'll cover the other steps as we go along. And, as you will see in the following chapters, there are lots of ways to "fuel" our minds. We will go over each of them at length and then expand on their use, implication, purpose, and value. Brain fuel comes in many forms, and each of us consumes that fuel in our own way at our own speed. The goal is to figure out a way to expand on the types of fuel we can efficiently consume and increase the rate at which we can consume that fuel.

Let's take a look at what that might look like now.

STEP 1 - BRAIN FUEL

UNLOCK YOUR INNER GENIUS - STEP 1 - BRAIN FUEL

To **Unlock your Inner Genius**, the first step is to unlock your Brain Fuel Profile. We must first determine how we prefer to receive information from the environment (people, computers, environmental noise). Everyone has a preference for receiving information, your unique **Brain Fuel**. This is your lens to the world, your learning lens, your input lens, your information lens.

To unlock our Brain Fuel Profile, we must first determine each different type of profile and unlock the core components and elements that make them work. In addition, the Brain Fuel profiles must be aligned with their derivatives and be aspirational, fun, and forward-thinking (related to future skill sets and our future world).

Once you know your Brain Fuel, you can learn quicker, switch gears to receive information given to make sense to you, and, best of all, reduce learning stress. It's pretty stressful for your brain to be in a 'learning state,' taking in information and sorting it out. So, if you can find out your Brain Fuel preference, then all of this becomes way easier.

UNLOCK YOUR INNER GENIUS - STEP 1 - FIND OUT YOUR BRAIN FUEL PREFERENCE

Luckily for you, we have cooked up a great way to help figure out exactly what your brain fuel preference is and how you can manipulate that information. The link below has some really awesome tips and tricks for all you aspiring genius learners. So give it a try now and see what you "think." You will not regret it!

www.innergeniusnow.com

BRAIN FUEL – THE WORLD THROUGH THE LENS OF LEARNING

WHAT IS MY UNIQUE LEARNING LENS?

Knowing your *Brain Fuel* preference brings your world into a new, sharp focus. Remember when you were about to purchase a new car, and you began to notice those exact cars on the road? Or, when you or a family member may have been diagnosed with a medical condition, and you begin to notice advertisements, articles, and groups supporting that condition? Or, perhaps you are studying sports medicine and begin to see sports through the lens of medicine. Then, you immediately start to focus on players' injuries and become alert to the medical conditions related to sports. It's a natural part of life.

"Where focus goes, energy flows," Tony Robbins says. "What you focus on, you feel." The power of focus affects all aspects of your life. You can focus on goals at work, in your relationships, or on personal goals like fitness and emotional health – and you can manifest those goals into being.

As soon as you discover your *Brain Fuel* preference, you'll naturally begin to notice your choice for taking in new information and how people are communicating with you. You'll naturally have a heightened focus on how you are learning, and others respond to your communication. Your unique learning preference is like a new lens to the world around you, and how you see and experience daily life will be enhanced.

ACTIVATING YOUR SENSORY LEARNING LENS: BRAIN FUEL

This step is related to kickstarting our senses and unlocking our "learning lens" to navigate the world. As such, let's take a look at how information gets into our heads and how learning takes place due to the direct transmission of data.

Data is relayed into our brains through our five senses: sight, sound, smell, taste, and touch. These are activated virtually instantly. We do not always think of our senses as avenues of learning, but they are a way for us to learn just as much as they are a way for us to experience the world around us. In fact, due to the intuitive nature of sensory input, we are primed to learn even when we might not be seeking it out.

Every sensory experience is a learning opportunity. When we perceive something new, we both experience that stimuli and form new stores of information that we could use either immediately or later.

For example, if you try a portion of new food, you might not describe it as such. Still, you *learned* that you like or dislike that food, what it tastes like, and now have new information to make decisions. Will I eat this again? Will I recommend it to someone else? How might I be able to leverage my new knowledge that *this* food tastes exactly the way it tastes? These are all highly valid questions to ask yourself after experiencing new inputs.

MODALITIES

Our senses lay the groundwork for several different ways people learn. We call these **modalities.** For example, perhaps you are a perfumer, a food scientist, an aromatherapist, or a sommelier. The sense of smell is likely a high-preference sense when it comes to new learning. On the other hand, suppose you are a food critic, a professional taste tester, a chef, or a food technologist. In that case, your tastebuds are at the front and center of your learning preference.

For most of us, though, our senses of sight, hearing, and touch are our dominant senses when learning new information. In short, it is what we see, what we hear, and what we do that fuels our learning.

Everyone has preferred sense, or perhaps two out of their five senses that are their optimum preference for new learning. For most learning situations, especially when it comes to school, business, or higher education, we eliminate smell and taste and look at people's sensory preferences based on sight, sound, and touch.

There are three types of learning styles based on the sensory intake' of information. **Visual** learners need to see the material to learn most effectively. **Auditory** learners learn best by hearing the material. **Kinesthetic** learners are those who learn best by doing. Most individuals use a combination of all three modalities. For example, suppose an individual is a strong visual learner but has good listening skills, too. In that case, that person may want to use those secondary auditory skills to boost the visual modality for even better learning. The kinesthetic response of rewriting notes after the lecture will help reinforce the material presented. How an individual takes in new information, sorts, retains, retrieves, and reproduces it depends heavily on their natural learning preference.

The three modalities are **visual, auditory, and kinesthetic**. Let's take a much closer look at each of them.

VISUAL LEARNERS – LEARN THROUGH SEEING

Visual learners can identify patterns in pictures, have a keen ability to distinguish shapes and colors using the naked eye, and have a good sense of organization.

VISUAL LEARNERS: HOW DO THEY LEARN BEST?

These learners may need to see the trainer's body language and facial expression to fully understand the content of a lesson. They tend to prefer sitting at the front of the classroom to avoid visual obstructions (e.g., people's heads). They may think in pictures and learn best from visual displays, including diagrams, illustrated textbooks, PowerPoint presentations, videos, flipcharts, and handouts. Visual learners often prefer to take detailed notes during a lecture or classroom discussion to absorb the information.

VISUAL LEARNERS: WEAKNESSES AND WATCH-OUTS

Conversely, they might struggle with large blocks of text. Instead, visual learners might prefer using a graph or watching a video to understand a new concept. Visual learners might also have difficulty with an audio-only transmission like a podcast.

AUDITORY LEARNERS – LEARN THROUGH LISTENING

Auditory learners learn best by the sense of hearing. However, talking is also counted as part of the auditory preference. People who prefer learning by hearing and speaking are exceptionally good at identifying patterns in music. They often appreciate storytelling as a means of teaching, are gifted at explaining things using simple language, and can easily follow directions. They are also good at identifying language patterns and are often better at learning new languages than their counterparts.

AUDITORY LEARNERS: HOW DO THEY LEARN BEST?

They learn best through verbal lectures, discussions, talking things through, and listening to what others have to say. Auditory learners interpret the underlying meanings of speech through listening to the tone of voice, pitch, speed, and other nuances.

Written information may have little meaning until it is heard. Therefore, these learners often benefit from reading text aloud and using a recording device.

AUDITORY LEARNERS: WEAKNESSES AND WATCH-OUTS

These learners have weaknesses like becoming easily distracted by fluctuations in ambient noise. They might also struggle to learn when it is entirely silent and might have difficulties learning from reading. Audiobooks are ideal for auditory learners who have difficulty using traditional textbooks.

KINESTHETIC LEARNERS – LEARN THROUGH DOING, MOVING, AND TOUCHING

For **Kinesthetic learners,** who we alluded to before, the optimal experience comes not from sights and sounds but from movement and physical activity. These learners often express themselves effectively using dance, are usually good at sports, and learn well by moving about in the space they seek to operate within.

KINESTHETIC LEARNERS: HOW DO THEY LEARN BEST?

Kinesthetic learners also understand things best when they can physically touch them. They like to use fine motor skills to feel textures, understand the size of things, etc. Some kinesthetic learners aren't focused on moving their bodies but learn simply by touching and manipulating things.

Kinesthetic, often called Tactile, learners learn best through a hands-on approach, actively exploring the physical world around them. They may find it hard to sit still for long periods and become distracted by their need for activity and exploration.

On the other hand, they frequently have difficulty during quiet learning or even test-taking and generally struggle in passive learning settings. It is much harder for kinesthetic learners to grasp theoretical concepts. It is much easier for them to learn by physically experiencing an idea.

These learners do well at retaining information from things like play and might struggle with text- and audio-based books.

KINESTHETIC LEARNERS: WEAKNESSES AND WATCH-OUTS

As you can imagine, some of these younger kinesthetic learners face challenges with traditional educational approaches that have dominated previous generations. In some cases, long ago, if a student could not retain what the teacher said during class or what they read during homework, they simply would not have learned the item.

Luckily, this is no longer the case, and there have been incredible advancements in educational theory surrounding these modalities. Extrapolating that research out, now both younger and older learners can benefit from figuring out which modality suits them and emphasizing it in their own experiences.

UNLOCK YOUR INNER GENIUS – STEP 1 – FIND OUT YOUR BRAIN FUEL PREFERENCE

Luckily for you, we have cooked up a great way to help figure out exactly what your brain fuel preference is and how you can manipulate that information. The link below has some excellent tips and tricks for all you aspiring genius learners. So, give it a try now and see what you "think." You will not regret it!

www.innergeniusnow.com

BRAIN FUEL IN ACTION

HOW CAN YOU HELP YOURSELF?

Let's put your Brain Fuel into Action. If you haven't already discovered your Brain Fuel profile, we suggest that you stop and complete it now.

www.innergeniusnow.com

USING YOUR BRAIN FUEL PROFILE TO LEARN QUICKER

So, you've discovered your **Brain Fuel Profile**. You're primarily powered by either, Visual, Auditory, or Kinesthetic. Indeed, we are all a combination of all three. In fact, we have to be. Information comes to us in all forms, and we have to adapt to however the incoming data is received. However, generally, everyone leans into one brain fuel type as their preference. The supercharged learner will translate a message or new information coming to them in a non-preferred way to their Brain Fuel Profile preference. Let's discover how that can be done!

BRAIN FUEL IN ACTION WHEN LEARNING

Listed here are some short-cuts and techniques for you to accelerate and **Unlock your Inner Genius**. When you go

91

through the list, focus on the column that is *your Brain Fuel profile*. We'll look at the others later.

When you are in a *learning situation*, use many of these methods to help you absorb the information faster. Then, regardless of how that information comes to you, you'll know how to 'translate' that information into your own Brain Fuel Preference.

BRAIN FUEL TECHNIQUES FOR LEARNING		
VISUAL	AUDITORY	KINESTHETIC
Find diagrams	Summarize material in your own words	Participate in activities that involve building, moving, or drawing
Sketch concepts and new information	Work in groups where discussions take place	Complete projects or act out stories
Schematics	Listen to other participant's viewpoints	Take a walk and listen to new learning as you walk
Photographs	Explain the concept or new material to someone	Take frequent breaks
Flow charts	Form a working team for discussion	Trace words with your finger
Visual representations of materials	Read aloud	Tap a pencil, shake your foot or hold onto something while learning
Reference books	Watch videos (you'll pick up on the voiceover)	Take notes on the computer
Videos or movies	Repeat key facts aloud	Keep doing things as you learn
List key points	Make up a rhyme or rap to remember key facts	Throw a ball as you recite new learnings

Enclose key points in boxes or circles	Record lessons and listen to them repeatedly	Build or sculpt a model of what you are learning
Draw lines between concepts to show connections	Sit where you can hear	Move, Move, Move
Color-code notes with a highlighter	Read stories, assignments, or directions out loud	Engage in an activity fully
Relate things of the same color	Repeat, Repeat, Repeat aloud	Get up and get involved
Draw pictures to help explain new concepts and then explain the pictures	Sing your study notes	Role play new learning

At this point, you are likely wondering how on earth it can be possible to organize all of these different concepts and techniques. Do we need all of them? Can I skip some?! The reality of the situation is that you do not need to leverage every single one of these techniques, nor do you need to incorporate everything we have discussed above into your daily learning routines.

There is a catch, though. You are here to supercharge your learning, **Unlock Your Inner Genius**, and you are here to push yourself to grow and adapt. In order to do those things, you are going to need to struggle a little bit. You are going to need to push yourself firmly into areas that may not be comfortable for you. It is completely normal to resist such discomfort, but you have to do it anyway!

Below, we will go over some ways that you can help ease the burden of this transition. Challenging yourself is hard, but ultimately you will find that a little bit of temporary pain can go a long way toward long-term success.

CHALLENGES, SOLUTIONS, AND AREAS FOR DEVELOPMENT

It might seem obvious, but so many people constantly multi-task while they are working. They have open social media apps, email, financial alerts, sports scores, and other avenues of information exchange while trying to absorb and retain new information. Unfortunately, this almost always leads to less productivity.

BRAIN FUEL CHALLENGES AND SOLUTIONS WHEN LEARNING		
VISUAL	AUDITORY	KINESTHETIC
Challenge – Gets distracted easily Solution – Avoid distractions while learning - turn off notifications and emails	Challenge – Gets distracted by noise Solution – Find a quiet place to learn	Challenge – Finds it hard to concentrate when reading large blocks of text Solution – Break up new information into chunks by physically highlighting sections

While it is tempting to try to accomplish many things at once, it is far more efficient to dedicate time to one item or another and take that task to completion. Furthermore, when we continually switch back and forth between tasks, we waste time refocusing our mental energy in the short breaks in between. It is akin to taking a small mental "tax" each time we move to another task.

Try to limit distractions of all kinds. This includes all Brain Fuel Profiles - Auditory, Visual, and Kinesthetic. Instead, focus your efforts on the consumption and processing of your brain fuel. If you want to supercharge and juice your learning, this is the best way to ensure you are giving yourself the best chance.

HOW CAN I SUPERCHARGE INTO MY INNER GENIUS ZONE?

It is entirely normal to have challenges when trying to absorb new information. Some people say, 'learning should be fun,' but nothing could be further from the truth for your brain. Your brain has to work super hard to make new pathways and forge those pathways to remember the new information, put it into use, and store it long term.

Let's look at your Brain Fuel Profile and some of the most frequent challenges. Then, think through each challenge, its solution, and how you can put that into action when you are in a learning situation.

BRAIN FUEL CHALLENGES AND SOLUTIONS WHEN LEARNING		
VISUAL	AUDITORY	KINESTHETIC
Often we are challenged with words and writing - spend time looking through the information and rewrite specific pieces	Sometimes we might be inclined to read slowly – it may be helpful to practice reading faster	Static lectures and being sedentary while learning is challenging - keep moving some part of your body while learning, no matter how slightly.
If it is hard to remember lists of words and numbers, invent symbols and categorize them into sections (recognize the importance of symbols!)	If you find complicated diagrams challenging to understand, try to get someone to explain them to you	In cases of hard-to-grasp concepts, practice and do it. Find the earliest opportunity to put learning into practice

BRAIN FUEL CHALLENGES AND SOLUTIONS WHEN LEARNING		
VISUAL	AUDITORY	KINESTHETIC
If it is hard to focus on long passages or written text, then spend time looking through the information and try to rewrite specific pages of information from memory	When there is difficulty understanding graphs and charts, transfer information into auditory forms	Have poor handwriting and difficulty spelling? Use computer processing power as much as possible and turn spell check on before communicating any written document
When there is difficulty understanding that context must be communicated, map out presentations in sequential steps, or use mind-mapping to find the visual, logical flow	Staying quiet for long periods can be challenging; take breaks or plan on having discussion activities	If you find tests and exams challenging, then practice writing the kinds of answers you will be expected to use in the examination— remember that the act of writing does seem to help information become more apparent to kinesthetic learners

THE IMPACT FOR YOU

Knowing what type of data input preference best suits you is essential if you are going to supercharge your learning experience. For the longest time, humans have had little or no say in how information was transmitted to them. Now, we know better, and we can give individuals the tools they need to learn in a way that suits their brain chemistry.

This is extremely important for a lot of reasons. One reason that is often overlooked is that we have the opportunity to not only **tailor our learning regimen to the mode of transmission** that best suits us. But we can also limit the instances in which we are being given information in a way that is not conducive to our learning preference.

Understanding the nuances of the different types of learning would have very likely been extremely useful for younger learners in generations past. But, unfortunately, that research simply did not exist until it did. You, though, have the luxury and the benefit of being able to take these learning considerations and put them to good use. Do not underutilize this opportunity.

SUMMARY

- Our senses lay the groundwork for several different ways people learn. We call these **Brain Fuel.**

- There are three types of Brain Fuel Profiles based on the sensory intake of information. **Visual** learners need to see the material to learn most effectively. **Auditory** learners learn best by hearing the material. Finally, **kinesthetic** learners are those who learn best by doing. Most individuals use a combination of all three modalities.

- **Visual learners** can identify patterns in pictures, have a keen ability to distinguish shapes and colors using the naked eye, and have a good sense of organization.

- **Auditory learners** learn best by the sense of hearing. However, talking is also counted as part of the auditory preference.

- For **Kinesthetic learners**, the optimal experience comes not from sights and sounds but from movement and physical activity.

LISTEN TO YOUR LANGUAGE, LISTEN TO YOUR LIFE

RECOGNIZING THE BRAIN FUEL OF PEOPLE AROUND YOU

Every day you'll encounter opportunities to communicate with other people. Now that you know your Brain Fuel Profile, you'll be learning quicker. This is because people who know their Brain Fuel Profile tailor their learning regimen to transmission mode.

The big questions are:

Can you be better when you're communicating with other people?

How do you communicate in a supercharged way?

What happens if they don't know their Brain Fuel Profile?

What if you could Unleash your Inner Genius and communicate with them in their Brain Fuel Profile, which may be different from yours?

The answer is now, "YOU CAN!"

BACK TO THE LEARNING LAB

In Neuro-Linguistic Programming (NLP) training, the senses through which we experience the world are referred to as representational systems.

The words used to describe these systems are called *predicates*.

Hence, you have several different systems working for you: **Visual predicates** (for things you see), **auditory predicates** (for something you hear), **kinesthetic predicates** (things you feel or tactile sensations), **olfactory predicates** (things you smell), and **gustatory predicates** (things you taste).

> *Predicate words and phrases are a simple form of imagery in your language that is used by people every day.*

Yes, listen to your family, friends, work colleagues, and you'll pick up their learning preferences just by listening to their language.

Okay, don't believe us?

Check out this list below and think about how many of these phrases you use regularly.

LIST OF PREDICATE PHRASES

Here you will find a complete list of predicate phrases.

You may recognize them in the way you talk or how friends, family, and colleagues talk.

The predicate phrases used naturally reveals a person's preference as a visual, auditory, kinesthetic, olfactory, or gustatory Brain Fuel.

VISUAL PREDICATES

People who have a **Visual Brain Fuel Profile** use Visual predicates when they communicate. These include, but are not limited to:

Seeing the bright side of things	Review	High regard	Out of sight
Clear overview	A feast for the eye	What kind of .... do you see yourself doing?	Can you imagine that?
Can you picture that?	Spotlighting	Insight	View
See	See-through	Show me	Tunnel vision
Vision	Perspective	Focus	Put you on the spot
Colorful	Uncover	Appear	Foreseen
Shiny	Brilliant	Sparkling	Illustrate
Picture me/this/yourself	Sharp	Color	Blurred
Bright/crystal clear	Have a clear picture	Clarify	A glow
In a glimpse	Eye to eye	Seeing in a larger context	Mental image
Spiritual Eye	Naked eye	Imagination (appealing to one's imagination)	Reflect
Photographic memory	Looks like a photo	Overseeing	Short-sighted
Visible	Demonstrate	Picturesque	Your true colors
It looks like it...	A mental image, a mental scene, in your mind's eye	With an eagle's eye	Keeping an eye on things
At first glance	Have an eye for something	That's illustrative for...	Let me take a look
Look, I mean...	Have an eye on	Against the background of	It is not so Black and White

101

Where does a lightbulb go on with you?	Show me what you mean. I see what you mean.	The problem stares at me in the face	Take a closer look
Hazing out in front	Beautiful to see	take a look here	This is a new perspective on...
What a dark subject!	Let us shine a light on this subject.	In the light of...	If I were to show you an attractive proposal, would you like to see whether it is what you want?
Wolf in sheep's clothing	What an oasis of peace	Through the eye of the needle	Sketching a rosy picture
Like two drops of water	Do you see a way to do that?	Turning a blind eye to something	Drop your eye on...

Both teachers and learners use these predicates for a variety of reasons. Visual imagery plays off the idea that you can relate to it and understand it if you can picture something. For example, we are all biologically driven by the idea that we want to be attractive to others. We also want to be around others who are attractive as well, and this urge drives a great deal of what we say and do.

When it comes to transmitting information, though, we can use this concept of attractiveness to our advantage, especially if we are communicating (or being communicated with) individuals that respond to visual predicates.

This is especially relevant in a business setting, as *painting* your work in an attractive *light* can be the difference between success and failure. For example, imagine you are pitching a story series to your editor at a newspaper. This editor is likely keen because news consumers have short attention spans and even shorter amounts of free time.

You would do well to illustrate the value of your news series by expressing its usefulness to the viewer regarding what they will see once the work is presented to them. In short, you want them to be attracted to the work, and you will need to convince your editor that they will be just that. One of the ways you can do this is by using visual predicates to drive home your point. Let your editor *draw* their own conclusions but be sure to *show* them just how appealing your work can be.

AUDITORY PREDICATES

People who have an **Auditory Brain Fuel Profile** use Auditory predicates when they communicate. These include, but are not limited to:

Questions	Talking	Voice	Outspoken
Calls	Shout	Say	That is what you are saying
I hear what you say	Be heard	Hear	Loud (and clear)
Screaming	Harmony	Melody	Chanting
Sound	Who sets the tone?	Hitting a different note	That sounds like...
Tuning/tuning in	It clicks	Roar	This is in harmony with...
Listening	A telling sign	Public voice	Said to be...
Just say...	Sounds good	Unheard of!	That doesn't tell me anything
Chattering	Describe in detail	that rings a bell	Talking to deaf ears
How does that sound to the ears?	Like music to the ears	Does it tell you something?	You are a chatterbox
I am all ears	Individual elements work together in harmony: they are the instruments for the verbal orchestra.	You say that...	Shout it from the rooftops

Auditory predicates are a great way to raise the stakes and bring attention to high-energy situations. These words and phrases naturally lend themselves to grabbing attention and not letting it go. For this reason, they work really well in things like marketing and advertising.

For example, let us pretend you are trying to sell a beverage product via an advertising buy on a local television network. The advertisement is aimed at young singles and is designed to portray fun, energy, and liveliness. To titillate your audience, you might want to deliver predicates that make their hearts *sing* to the *beat* of the night. You want them to hear the music at the beach, hear the beat drop at the club and hear the *rhythm* of the product.

Sounds are exciting, and they are often associated with exciting events. Concerts, crowds, soundtracks, and even emergencies and danger all have strong tonal elements. Therefore, communicating in this way is extremely useful in a lot of instances.

KINESTHETIC PREDICATES

People who have a **Kinesthetic Brain Fuel Profile** use Kinesthetic predicates when they communicate. These include, but are not limited to:

I feel that...	Cold / Warm	Heated (heated debate)	Hold on to that idea
Heartwarming	Heartbreaking	Feel	Slowly...
Wet	Firmly	Solid	Weight
Balanced	Light-footed	Holding on to	Gripping
Transform to	Moving someone around	I have the feeling that	Support
Tangibly	Grasp (Getting a grasp on...)	Slipped through your fingers	Moving
Search for trigger points	Connect with	Throw it out	In concrete terms

Scraping	Keeps on sticking	Whip up	I feel what you are saying
Feels good	Crushing	It comes down to	Tackling the issue
Keying up	Well-founded	Get in touch with	Hand in hand
Persevere	Keeping your foot on the ball	Underlining on	Reverse world
Balanced	Applying pressure	To twist	To pivot
To flex	Change tracks	Switch gears	Falling
Impression	Touched	Stirring	Clamped
Relaxed	Sensitive	Razor-sharp	Striking
Overpowered	Insensitive	Hard	Soft
Let's stay in touch	Where does it create a familiar feeling for you?	Walking into something	If I make you a concrete proposal, you can experience for yourself whether it feels good or not.
Hold on to	Creating a basis for	Have a handle	Pulling the strings
Feel good in your skin	The pressure is off	Pressure	I couldn't put my finger on it
Tell me something interesting, and I'm hanging on to your lips ('Yes, I still feel it!').	A stab in the back	Keep our spines straight.	Always keep the door open.
It feels like a warm blanket (of...)	It disappears like ice in a hot oven.	I felt like I had to walk on eggshells.	

Kinesthetic predicates might be the most fun to explore. They help make abstract concepts and make them into *concrete* concepts that are easy to *grasp* and *hold* onto. In addition, these predicates are very helpful when dealing with individuals who make their living by getting their *hands dirty* and putting a little elbow grease into their work.

These predicates are great when trying to relate to people on an emotional level; this is largely because they provide a sense of commonality and comfort. When we talk about how we *feel*, it often evokes an emotional response concerning how we might be feeling inside. This connection can be strong and valuable.

For example, if you were writing a story, you would very likely be leaning heavily on the use of kinesthetic predicates to put the reader in the place of the story's characters. As such, these phrases offer an excellent conduit for communicating aesthetics. Again, this is absolutely critical when it comes to storytelling.

OLFACTORY AND GUSTATORY PREDICATES

Bitter	Stinking	Unsavory	Fragrant
To my taste	Sweet	It is right under your nose	You smell danger
Seasoning it with humor	Tasteful	Gourmet	Smelly

Many of these are a little more unusual than the other predicates we mentioned above, but that does not mean they do not have a place in our interactions and communication. We tend to use these predicates more sparingly, but done effectively, they can really deliver a powerful message.

One widely applicable and extremely popular predicate is the simple designation that something is *sweet*. This works wonders in a romantic setting, and in fact, this concept is so *potent* that it is borderline cliché. However, you might use these predicates when composing a love letter, writing a song, or penning a poem. Each of those is ripe for this sort of predicate action.

WHAT CAN YOU EXPECT TO ACHIEVE BY USING PREDICATE PHRASES?

As super-charged humans who have **Unlocked Their Inner Genius**, we can build rapport, either in-person or digitally, by speaking using phrases according to everyone's preferred system of language. Using insightful and purposeful language creates keys for the person in their preferred predicates, and it's not long to wait before another appeals to their preference. Most of the time, people are unaware of the method of using predicate phrases. It simply feels like the person (the one that has unlocked their *Inner Genius*) is 'speaking their language.'

With visualizations and stories, you can use predicates to make them more vivid. For a more substantial effect, insert adjectives before the V, A, K, O, or G words for a more substantial effect. For example, you can *see blue eyes*, or you can *see sparkling crystal blue eyes*.

Another application is simply to make your speech more spectacular, instead of boring company language. Otherwise, your employees will fall asleep. Martin Luther King worked with all the senses all the time.

> *"There are so many opportunities*
> *in life that you can just taste them.*
> *You have to grab them."*

UNLEASHING YOUR INNER GENIUS EVERYDAY

So, you might be asking yourself, how can I apply this information in my own day-to-day interaction?. This is a great question and one we are going to spend a little time answering now. The most important thing to keep in mind when considering which predicates to use (or not to use) is that everyone, including ourselves, leans toward one set or another. That's our *Brain Fuel* in action!

When we are trying to communicate a message to someone else, we might be using one set of predicates or another, which might be boosting or hampering our efforts. Individuals who have not fully **Unlocked Their Inner Genius** might have a hard time identifying if they are failing or succeeding with respect to their predicate usage. If you know what you are looking to do, you can pivot your messaging accordingly. If, on the other hand, you are unaware of how these predicates play in the minds of those you are communicating with, you will be unable to mitigate communications problems arriving from missed cues.

Additionally, having a grasp of these predicate cues can also help you when you are struggling to receive a message. Perhaps the teacher, trainer, presenter, or boss does not know which clues will hit the mark for you and which ones will not. So long as you understand why you might not be on the same page as the communicator, you can restructure the interaction to better suit your needs. In other words, knowing what you do not know (or what doesn't look, sound, or feel right) is just as important as knowing what you do know!

THE IMPACT FOR YOU

Knowledge, they say, is power. This is probably a more literal statement than initially realized because knowing how to utilize predicate action is one of the best ways to impact both the office and home. However, I'd like to suggest changing this quote to:

> *"Knowledge is power, but only if you use it!"*

This, too, is a two-way street. Learners benefit from understanding where their strengths and shortcomings lie for specific language decisions, and communicators benefit from using targeted, particular language to best express themselves and rely on critical content.

You will likely be a teacher and a learner, in one capacity or another, at many points in your educational journey. Being able to parse through complex language nuances like the ones described above is extremely useful. Practice this every day, work diligently toward mastery and always keep predicate action in the back of your head!

SUMMARY

- Predicate phrases are naturally occurring language patterns that can reveal someone's learning preference.

- We all use **visual predicates** (for things you see), **auditory predicates** (for things you hear), **kinesthetic predicates** (things you feel or tactile sensations), **AD or self-talk predicates** (also called labeling systems), **olfactory predicates** (things you smell), and **gustatory predicates** (things you taste) in our everyday language. So listen out for it – these phrases are everywhere!

- Some people prefer one type of predicate over another.

- **Visual predicates** and imagery play off the idea that you can relate to it and understand it if you can picture something.

- **Auditory predicates** are a great way to raise the stakes and bring attention to high-energy situations. These words and phrases naturally lend themselves to grabbing attention and not letting it go. For this reason, they work really well in things like marketing and advertising.

- **Kinesthetic predicates** might be the most fun to explore. They help make abstract concepts and make them into *concrete* ideas that are easy to *grasp* and *hold* onto.

- **Olfactory and gustatory predicates** might be used to compose a love letter, write a song, or pen a poem.

- When we are trying to communicate a message to someone else, we might be using one set of predicates or another, which might be bosting or hampering our efforts. Individuals who have unlocked their inner genius will be better at identifying if they are failing or succeeding in their predicate usage.

BALANCE YOUR COMMUNICATION TO MATCH OTHER'S BRAIN FUEL PREFERENCES

NOW YOU KNOW YOUR BRAIN FUEL – WHAT'S NEXT?

Here, we will cover the different ways information can be packaged. These are the brain fuel cells, so to speak. And some of the ways that information can be used and manipulated. The aim here is to unlock the learning for other people. By using a series of **Brain Fuel Keys**, we can do just that. Let's explore more!

Let's look at *(did you notice that predicate phrase?)* some of the ways these pieces of information are packaged in academic, business learning and development, meetings, or other group settings. This is a broad and diverse list, and it features many strategies that have proven helpful in various settings. But, almost certainly, you will have already been exposed to many of these in your own educational travels.

'BRAIN FUEL KEYS' TO HELP WHEN TEACHING OR PRESENTING

As a teacher, trainer, facilitator, presenter, or manager, some of these "keys" may have already proven successful for you. Some might be new, while others might not be your cup of tea. There are so many ways of incorporating **all Brain Fuel Profiles** into every lesson, presentation, session or meeting, that you'll find the combination that both suits your presentation style and provides balance for all profiles. What you need is a **set of keys to unlock everyone's Brain Fuel**.

If you are a parent, a sports coach, co-worker, friend, partner, in fact, anyone, read on! We are all communicating knowledge every day. Regardless of your capacity as a teacher or educator, you can use the following skills to ignite communication and spark learning to whomever you are speaking or writing.

STRATEGY 1 - LEARN TO USE OTHER PEOPLE'S PREDICATE PHRASES

The first strategy that you've already learned is to use other people's predicate phrases. Learning just a few of the predicate phrases discussed earlier will help you pivot your communication into *their* Brain Fuel Profile.

STRATEGY 2 - BALANCE YOUR COMMUNICATION

The second strategy is to balance your communication. To balance your training session, lesson, presentation, coaching session, talk, or meeting means incorporating methods and activities (keys) that suit all three Brain Fuel Profiles, not just yours. This means that regardless of who participates, the **Brain Fuel keys** will be there for them. This is a very clever idea because then everyone has an equal opportunity to accelerate their learning. Furthermore, you'll find that you are more engaging as a facilitator/trainer/presenter/general communicator. People who participate will actually participate, not just sit there and listen.

Brain Fuel Key – a method of communication or activity that unlocks the learning of Visual, Auditory, or Kinesthetic Brain Fuel Profiles.

Consider some of these keys below and reflect on your experiences with them so far.

BRAIN FUEL KEYS		
VISUAL	AUDITORY	KINESTHETIC
Animation	Debate	Building models
Color participant guides	Expert panel	Competitions
Colored markers	Group discussion	Drawing flowcharts
Diagrams	Guest speakers (specifically, subject matter experts)	Field trips
Draw icon, graphic, symbol activities	Interview	Frequent breaks
Flipchart activities & present back	Mini-lectures	Hands-on activities
Flipcharts with key content	Music	Move participants around the room after each break
Flowcharts & diagrams	Present back key learnings	Pacing back and forth
Handouts	Read aloud	Presentation of key learnings
Movies	Record lectures for repeated listening	Projects
Pictures	Say directions	Real-life examples
PowerPoint™ slideshow	Talk about illustrations and diagrams in texts	Repeat back directions

See parts of words	Talk through problems; paraphrase ideas about new concepts	Role-Playing
Study cards and flashcards	Think, pair, share	Self-discovery (rather than set directions)
Suitable pictures & graphics	Use mnemonic devices	Small group activities
Timelines	Use rhymes to help memorize	Underlining notes
Use clue words for recalling	With new processes, talk about what to do, how to do it, and why it's done that way	Whole Group Activities
Use color and consistent color coding		
Video		
Wallcharts with quotes		
Watch TV		
Write down directions		

PUTTING BRAIN FUEL KEYS INTO ACTION

There are lots of ways these Brain Fuel Keys can be composed. Here we will go over a few of the most common ways that they are described and some of the specific ways you can incorporate Brain Fuel Keys into every conversation, every talk, presentation, teaching, or coaching session – in fact, every time you communicate!

For example, in a one-hour meeting presentation, consider incorporating the following Brain Fuel Keys:

INCORPORATE VISUAL BRAIN FUEL KEYS

Firstly, focus on your refining the PowerPoint slides that you share during the presentation. Are they addressing the Visual Brain Fuel participants? Check that they are full of color and relevant pictures, preferably photographs over clipart. Perhaps you could incorporate a timeline or a diagram. Or, stop after a few minutes and have people work in groups to create a symbol or icon for the content that you've just presented.

INCORPORATE AUDITORY BRAIN FUEL KEYS

Next, check your Auditory Brain Fuel Keys. If you are the presenter, practice giving specific directions to make sure your language is clear and quickly followed. Next, perhaps play music as everyone enters the room, even if it's a virtual meeting. Or, stop after a few minutes, have people pair up, share their key learnings, and then present them back to the whole group.

INCORPORATE KINESTHETIC BRAIN FUEL KEYS

If you are teaching or presenting in the exact geographic location as your participants, adding a Kinesthetic Brain Key like working in groups to build a model of what you are teaching is straightforward. If you are working virtually, then you might devise a competition where the 'buzzer' to answer a question is something that the participants create using what they have around them (e.g., using a pen to tap on the glass, shaking a pencil case, or beating a marker on their desk). Remember that the most straightforward **Kinesthetic Brain Key** is to get people to go outside, think about the main things that they've learned, write them down and resume the session to share their thoughts.

None of these ideas take much time, little preparation, and almost always zero cost. However, every time you consider placing a Brain Fuel Key into what you are presenting or teaching, you skyrocket the possibility for getting the attention from that Brain Key Profile.

TASKS FOR EACH BRAIN FUEL PROFILE

Previously, we covered *Predicate Phrases,* and by now, you've probably noticed people around you speaking those very words. Of course, it's pretty awesome to uncover other people's Brain Fuel by listening carefully to the words they use. But, what about when it comes to you communicating a task that will balance your meeting, written communication, presentation, or training program beautifully so that those Brain Fuel Keys really fire?

The following table is a **short-cut of tasks** that you can assign to attendees and participants to quickly key them in. Even without any pre-thought, you could do this on the fly. For example, let's say you have a Visual Brain Fuel profile. You'll most likely be talking in your Visual predicate phrase language – keying Visual Brain Fuelers in, but what about the Auditory and Kinesthetic Brain Fuelers? Keep this Fast-track Brain Fuel Key Lexicon at the ready. This will help you to quickly assign a task with little preparation. For example, when you feel like your presentation needs some unlocking to key into people's profiles, refer to this Fast-track Brain Fuel Lexicon and quickly assign the group or individual a task. Too easy!

FAST-TRACK BRAIN FUEL LEXICON		
VISUAL	**AUDITORY**	**KINESTHETIC**
Color-coding	Describe	Simulations
Color-oriented	Discuss	Hands-on Environment
Concept maps	Explain	Tactile Learning
Diagram	Extroverted	Drawing
Envision imagery	Lecture	Building
Graphics	Listening	Full-body Movement
Look	Music	Practice
Reading	Sing	Movement
Reflect	Sound out words	Write notes
Slideshows	State	Create
To-do lists	Talk	Build
Visual Aids	Talk through	Compare
Visualize	Verbal Praise	Model

Additionally, it is useful to remember that you do not need to rely on anyone in particular to create Brain Fuel, nor do you need anyone to inject that fuel for you. In a lot of ways, you can help yourself. In fact, the more aggressive you are at seeking out Brain Fuel and consuming that fuel, the better you are going to be.

THE IMPACT FOR YOU

When you Unlock your Inner Genius and know your Brain Fuel, you'll be learning at an increased rate, and whatever you are learning will be less of a struggle. As you **tailor your learning regimen to the mode of transmission,** you will become like a professional language interpreter, taking in one mode and translating to another.

But, when you can balance your communication during meetings and presentations so that everyone's Brain Fuel is unlocked with your powerful communication keys – well, that's a whole new world. You'll find people are paying more attention to what you are presenting. They'll be more engaged, they'll say to you afterward, 'everything made sense,' or, 'that was fantastic.' This is their language as participants, students, and attendees. What they are really saying is, 'you used incredible communication power to make it seem like the message was explicitly built for me. By using these keys, you are now in a position to **tailor your teaching/presenting/communication regimen to unlock all modes of transmission.** This is a game-changer for them and for you!

SUMMARY

- There are so many ways of incorporating all Brain Fuel Profiles into every lesson, presentation, session or meeting, that you'll find the combination that both suits your presentation style and provides balance for all profiles. What you need is a set of keys to unlock everyone's Brain Fuel.

- The first strategy is to use Predicate Phrases

- The second strategy is to balance your communication.

- Brain Fuel Key – a method of communication or activity that unlocks the learning of Visual, Auditory, or Kinesthetic Brain Fuel Profiles.

- There are lots of ways these Brain Fuel Keys can be incorporated into every conversation, every talk, presentation, teaching, or coaching session – in fact, every time you communicate!

- When you feel like your presentation needs some unlocking to key into people's profiles, refer to the Fast-track Brain Fuel Key Lexicon and quickly assign the group or individual a task.

STEP 2 - PROCESSING POWER

Here, we will discuss the next step in our four-step approach to amped-up and efficient learning and communication. We will now visit the "super freeway of learning," which comprises the Processing Powers: **Connect, Detail, Construct, Invent**.

These four **Processing Powers** allow us to take the Brain Fuel we consumed and whip it into something useful. Information that is not appropriately processed does us little good, so we must synthesize that information efficiently.

Again, and you will notice this is a theme in modern education theory, there is more than one way for this processing to occur. And you will also see, again, each of us has different strengths when it comes to deploying our Processing Power. In the section below, we will parse through some of the ways different people engage with their brain fuel and what the impacts of those engagements will be. We will also touch upon some notable individuals who fit the other kind of processing profiles.

Like you saw with Brain Fuel, there are two angles: how to unlock your own profile and unlock other people. It's just the same for Processing Power. Firstly, recognize how you can unlock your own *Inner Genius* by utilizing your Processing Power to its most significant advantage. Then, turn the tables and discover the possibilities when communicating, teaching, coaching, presenting, and talking to other people. It's a little trickier than Brain Fuel Keys, but the Processing Power keys are available to you. It's there, right in front of you every time you speak to another human.

So, let's firstly understand each of the four Processing Powers: **Connect, Detail, Construct, Invent!**

UNLOCK YOUR INNER GENIUS – STEP 2 – FIND OUT YOUR PROCESSING POWER

Luckily for you, we have devised a sensational way to help figure out exactly what your Processing Power Preference is and how you can use that information today, tomorrow and every day for the rest of your life! The link below has some elegant tips and tricks for all you aspiring genius learners and communicators. So give it a try now and see what you "process." You will not regret it!

<u>www.innergeniusnow.com</u>

CONNECT

PEOPLE WITH CONNECT AS THEIR PROCESSING POWER: WHO ARE THEY?

People who have the preference to process information as **Connect** are unique, interesting, and engaging. They want to know the reason for learning and need to identify a reason to learn. When they are stuck and can't connect, they will find a reason to engage and connect with the topic they are learning or discussing. They magically bring together the past and their present situation to truly understand. And they recognize their current knowledge to engage in more learning. They have a need to contribute their perspective, be heard, and be recognized for it.

KEY ATTRIBUTES - CONNECT
Want to know the reason for learning
Identify a reason to learn
Find a reason to engage with the topic
Focus on past and present understanding
Recognize current knowledge and engage in more learning
Contribute to individual's perspective

This Processing Power is also a global learner, and as such, prefers learning by observing the big picture. They learn in chunks and are holistic. They absorb materials almost randomly without seeing connections, then suddenly "get it" and quickly solve complex problems. Once **Connect** learners have grasped the big picture, they can put things together in novel ways but may not explain how they did it. Some people report that they have discovered they have **Connect Processing Power** yet think they are sequential learners. Generally, this is false. They have strong sequential abilities AFTER they've grasped the big picture, which puts them in the category of a global learner.

HOW CAN I UNLOCK MY INNER GENIUS PROCESSING POWER – CONNECT

Start today! When you are learning something new, you can **tailor your learning regimen to the mode of transmission.** But, regardless of your Brain Fuel, once you've received the new information, it's time for processing. So, use these methods to Unlock your Inner Genius by transforming the information into something that works for you!

UNLOCK YOUR INNER GENIUS
WII-FM questions
Demonstration
Mind mapping
Brainstorming
Make a logo
Imagery
Discuss meaning and relevance with others

FAMOUS PEOPLE IN THE CLASS OF CONNECT

Aristotle
Bill Gates
Confucius
Mahatma Gandhi
Malala Yousafzai
Martin Luther King
Sigmund Freud
Stephen Hawking

SHORT-CUT KEYS THAT YOU CAN USE TODAY TO UNLOCK YOUR INNER GENIUS

The following table is a **short-cut of tasks** that you can use to Unlock your Inner Genius and power your own learning. Keep this Fast-track Processing Power Lexicon at the ready. When processing new information, think about how you can extend your learning. As a **Connect PP,** think about how you can connect with other people to collaborate, have discussions, build meaning, share personal experiences, explore What's In It for Me (WII-FM), and other ways to connect the new information into your world. Too easy!

CONNECT - FAST-TRACK PROCESSING POWER LEXICON
Collaboration
Discussion
Feeling
Humanize
Meaning
Personal experience
Personal Incentive
Personify
Trust
Ask Why?
WII-FM (What's In It For Me)

THE IMPACT FOR YOU (ISN'T THAT IMPORTANT FOR YOU AS A CONNECT PP?)

When you Unlock your Inner Genius and know that your Processing Power is **Connect** you'll be learning at an increased rate. Whatever you are learning will be less of a struggle. You'll be able to relate your learning to your own experience and think about the benefit, the advantage, and the meaning of what you are learning. As you **tailor your**

learning regimen to the mode of transmission, you will be able to use the methods to quickly take new information and put it into a process that works for you.

SUMMARY

- People who have the preference to process information as **Connect** are unique, interesting, and engaging.

- This Processing Power is also a global learner, and as such, prefers learning by observing the big picture. Therefore, they learn in chunks and are holistic.

- As a Connect PP, think about how you can connect with other people to collaborate, have discussions, build meaning, share personal experiences, explore What's In It for Me (WII-FM), and other ways to connect the new information into your world.

- Keep practicing. Once you know your personal Inner Genius keys, you'll unlock a new world of possibilities in the way you learn, communicate, interact and stand out in the world.

UNLOCKING PEOPLE WHO HAVE 'CONNECT PP'

As we have said before, knowing who you are, how you best process information is an excellent accelerator to **Unlocking your Inner Genius**. However, the real power is when you discover how to **Unlock the Inner Genius of others**. So, let's find out how you can use your Inner Genius Keys to unlock the potential for people with the Connect Processing Power.

KEY QUESTION - CONNECT

Is there one question that you can immediately tap into, expedite, and drive communication with those with the **Connect** Processing Power?

Imagine if there was one question that would **Connect** you to people that are not like you. Does that exist?

Luckily, yes. Ask this one **Key Question** to tap into and **Connect:**

> *What's your experience with [this topic]?*

Say you are coaching a basketball player and doing drills to develop the team's shooting ability. You'd ask: *'What's your experience with drills?'*

Let's say you're presenting new budget information to your team at work. You'd ask: '*What's your experience in reading a profit and loss?*'

Or, you're teaching someone to learn a new piece of computer equipment that does 3D printing. You'd ask: '*What's your experience with XYZ printers that do 3D printing?*'

You might be thinking that if people are learning, they will probably all say the same thing, 'nothing.' But nothing could be further from the truth. They'll expand and tell you what they already know and expand the conversation so that you can ask further questions to **Connect** even more. Try it out – you might be amazed at the outcomes.

When you ask this **Key Question**, people who have a preference to process their information using Connect will skip a beat. It's like you've just opened their soul and are talking directly to them. So remember, once you've asked this question, stop, listen and get ready to ask more questions to **Connect.**

PROCESSING POWER KEYS USED WHEN TEACHING OR PRESENTING

Given that people with the Connect Processing Power are all about finding meaning and building interaction, it makes sense that when you are teaching, presenting, coaching, or communicating with them, activities and methods (the keys) is about Connecting.

PROCESSING POWER KEYS - CONNECT
Activities to build human interaction
Activities to build respect
Activities to build trust
Conversations about the possible meaning
Discussion
Finding the 'big idea.'

How do you feel about the learning?
Link to personal values
Personal meaning, not meaning for others
Personal, meaningful connections based on experience
Putting the topic into context
Shared storytelling to find out the meaning
The attention grabber - tell them why

SHORT-CUT TASKS THAT YOU CAN USE TODAY

The following table is a **short-cut of tasks** you can assign to attendees and participants to quickly key them in. Even without any pre-thought, you could do this on the fly. For example, let's say c a *Connect Processing Power*. You'll most likely be very comfortable engaging in activities such as partnering, collaboration, and finding meaning.

Keep this Fast-track Processing Power Lexicon at the ready. This will help you to quickly assign a task with little preparation. For example, when you feel like your presentation needs some unlocking to key into people's profiles, refer to this Super List and quickly assign the group or individual a task. Too easy!

CONNECT - FAST-TRACK PROCESSING POWER LEXICON
Collaboration
Discussion
Feeling
Humanize
Meaning
Personal experience
Personal Incentive
Personify
Trust
Ask Why?
WII-FM (What's In It For Me)

KEY QUESTION CHECKLIST

After each time you present, train, coach, facilitate or converse, and just before you press 'send' on the next email you write, check to ensure that you have used your Connect PP Keys. Just before you finish, did you...?

DID I....
Articulate the reason why?
Create an opportunity to buy in?
Recognize previous experience?
Link to personal values?

KEY WORDS TO SPRINKLE INTO YOUR LANGUAGE

When communicating with people who have the preference to process information as **Connect,** use connecting language. The benefit is that they'll feel like you are 'talking their language.'

WORDS TO COMMUNICATE WITH/TO THIS PROCESSING POWER

Additional benefit	Advantage	Advantageousness
Asset	Belief	Benefit
Context	Definition	Drift
Explanation	Feeling	Focus
Gain	Goal	Heart
Idea	Implication	Impression
Intention	Justification	Meaning
Merit	Motivation	Nuance
Perspective	Point	Position
Prior knowledge	Purpose	Return
Reward	Reward	Sense
Significance	Slant	Spirit
Strength	Symbolization	Understanding
Upside	Usefulness	Value
View	Viewpoint	Way of thinking
Whole idea	Worth	Worthiness

THE IMPACT FOR YOU

A connection has value both in an intellectual capacity as well as a human capacity. By facilitating a relationship with those who exhibit these features, regardless of if you fall into this profile, you will be strengthening one of the core values needed to supercharge learning on a social, emotional, and cognitive level. This is really a magnificent learning profile for all parties involved!

For those of you out there with this profile, remember that you wield a great deal of power. Thinking, on a very fundamental level, hinges on making connections. This takes place both between one's mental processes and considerations *and* with those around them. Learning is social. So is thinking. The Connector is at a significant advantage in this respect.

SUMMARY

- Connectors are primarily concerned with the question: What's your experience with [this topic]?

- They thrive on building trust, communication, and interaction with others.

- These learners are solid collaborators and are excellent when thrust into a group or social setting.

DETAIL

PEOPLE WITH DETAIL AS THEIR PROCESSING POWER: WHO ARE THEY?

People who have the preference to process information as **Detail** are often misunderstood. They can come off as cold and calculating. However, in truth, they also still possess an excellent capacity for subjective thought and even creativity. The difference is that their minds are wired to sift complex data out first, and they often tend to act on that complex data with conviction and expediency. Do not mistake this profile, though, as one that inhibits problem-solving and generating new thought pathways; these thinkers are very capable of just that. The only difference is that their first instincts pull them toward facts and figures, and those take precedent to building solutions.

KEY ATTRIBUTES - DETAIL
Wants to get the facts and concepts
Formulates concepts about topics
Congruent structures and processes

One great thing about **Detail** learners and thinkers is their propensity to sort through complex data and find relevant, actionable pieces of information efficiently. This is a really great skill to have, and one that is especially important, for example, for tasks rooted in science and math. Unfortunately, fact-based learning might have been over-utilized in the early days of education. Still, there will always be a role in problem-solving for individuals who can cut through large swaths of data to find helpful information. **Detail** processors are just the people for that type of work.

HOW CAN I UNLOCK MY INNER GENIUS PROCESSING POWER – DETAIL

Start today! When you are learning something new, we can **tailor our learning regimen to the mode of transmission.** But, regardless of your Brain Fuel, once you've received the new information, it's time for processing. So, use these methods to Unlock your Inner Genius by transforming the information into something that works for you!

UNLOCK YOUR INNER GENIUS
Lecture
Timelines
Charts
Graphs
Make a logo
Example of the finished product
Step-by-step processes
Flowcharts
Pictures

FAMOUS PEOPLE IN THE CLASS OF DETAIL

Amanda Gorman
J K Rowling
Jane Austin
Nicola Sturgeon
Serena Williams
Sheryl Sandberg
Susan Rice
Warren Buffet

SHORT-CUT KEYS THAT YOU CAN USE TODAY TO UNLOCK YOUR INNER GENIUS

The following table is a **short-cut of tasks** that you can use to Unlock your Inner Genius and power your own learning. Keep this Fast-track Processing Power Lexicon at the ready. When processing new information, think about how you can extend your learning. As a **Detail PP, think about maximizing** your strength for analysis and detail and how you can help others who do not share your strengths.

DETAIL - FAST-TRACK PROCESSING POWER LEXICON
Analytical
Concepts
Data
Detail
Facts
Formulating ideas
Learning what experts think
Processes
Statistics
Step-by-step
Thinking

THE IMPACT FOR YOU – THE DETAIL

When you Unlock your Inner Genius and know that your Processing Power is **Detail,** you'll be learning at an increased rate, and whatever you are learning will be less of a struggle. You'll be able to dig into the details, analyze facts, data, and statistics with ease. As you **tailor your learning regimen to the mode of transmission,** you will be able to use the methods to quickly take new information and put it into a process that works for you.

SUMMARY

- Detailers might sometimes come off as cold and calculating, but in truth, they possess a great capacity for subjective thought and creativity.

- Their first cognitive instincts pull them toward facts and figures, and those take precedent with respect to building solutions.

- Detail processors can cut through large swaths of data to find useful information and are strongly suited for that kind of work.

UNLOCKING PEOPLE WHO HAVE 'DETAIL PP'

As we have said before, knowing who you are, how you best process information is an excellent accelerator to **Unlocking your Inner Genius**. However, the real power is when you discover how to **Unlock the Inner Genius of others**. So, let's find out how you can use your Inner Genius Keys to unlock the potential for people with the **Detail** Processing Power.

KEY QUESTION - DETAIL

Is there one question that you can immediately tap into, expedite, and drive communication with those with the **Detail** Processing Power?

Imagine if there was one question that would **Detail** you to people that are not like you. Does that exist?

Luckily, yes. Ask this one **Key Question** to tap into and **Detail:**

What are the facts?

The facts are always important. All learning is rooted, in one way or another, in an objective, measurable premises. Detail profilers are keenly attuned to identifying these premises and excel in promulgating them as well.

To tap into this well, ask questions like: "Have you tested this premise?" Or maybe, "Can this data be measured?"

Again, you may be thinking that you will get a lot of overlap in the responses and that overlap is going to sound a lot like "nothing." But that really is not the case. They'll expand and tell you what they already know and expand the conversation so that you can ask further questions to Detail even more.

When you ask this Key Question, people who have a preference to process their information using Detail will be quick to answer. You will feel the information flow from them, so naturally, it will be truly remarkable. Remember, once you've asked this question, stop, listen and get ready to ask more questions to Detail.

PROCESSING POWER KEYS USED WHEN TEACHING OR PRESENTING

Given that people with the Detail Processing Power are all about finding raw, actionable data and consuming it, it makes sense that when you are teaching, presenting, coaching, or communicating with their activities and methods (the keys) are about Detailing.

PROCESSING POWER KEYS - DETAIL
Focus on relating and organizing information
Focus on remembering and reciting
Get straight to the point
Information orientation
Lectures (teaching)

SHORT-CUT TASKS THAT YOU CAN USE TODAY

The following table is a **short-cut of tasks** that you can assign to attendees and participants to quickly key them in. Even without any pre-thought, you could do this on the fly.

Keep this Fast-track Processing Power Lexicon at the ready. This will help you to quickly assign a task with little preparation. For example, when you feel like your presentation needs some unlocking to key into people's profiles, refer to this Super List and quickly assign the group or individual a task. Too easy!

DETAIL - FAST-TRACK PROCESSING POWER LEXICON
Analytical
Concepts
Data
Detail
Facts
Formulating ideas
Learning what experts think
Processes
Statistics
Step-by-step
Thinking

KEY QUESTION CHECKLIST

After each time you present, train, coach, facilitate or converse, and just before you press 'send' on your next email, check to ensure that you have used your Detail PP Keys. Just before you finish, did you...?

DID I....
Explain the data/steps/process clearly?
Have a stepwise plan for execution?
Equip people with all knowledge and information needed?

KEY WORDS TO SPRINKLE INTO YOUR LANGUAGE

When communicating with people who have the preference to process information as **Detail,** use connecting language. The benefit is that they'll feel like you are 'talking their language.'

Actuality	Approach	Basic
Blueprint	Bottom line	Chapter and verse
Concrete information	Cornerstone	Defend
Define	Degree	Describe
Detail	Evidence	Explain
Fact-based	Foundation	Generalize
Identify	Illustrate	Increment
Label	Layout	List
Match	Method	Number of
Paraphrase	Part	Principle
Proof	Reality	Recite
Recognize	Relate	Restate
Review	Size	Standard
Statistic	Substance	Summarize
Tell	Transaction	Truth
What		

THE IMPACT FOR YOU

Detailing is extremely helpful in instances when individuals are expected to synthesize large amounts of complex data. They are wonderful additions to any panel, task force, committee or focus group that might have to grapple with experimentation, quantitative analysis and many other math and science related considerations.

Do not shy away from the Detailer, even if they may appear distant and stoic. This is simply a result of their mind focusing on complex problem-solving! Detailers offer great value and benefits even in groups settings, so be sure to speak their language whenever you are working with or educating one of them!

SUMMARY

- To tap into the Detail PP, ask questions like: "Have you tested this premise?"

- Detail profilers are keenly attuned to identifying these premises, and excel in promulgating them as well.

- Detailers are most likely to be very comfortable when engaging in activities such as focused studying, reading tables, and visualizing charts

CONSTRUCT

PEOPLE WITH CONSTRUCT AS THEIR PROCESSING POWER: WHO ARE THEY?

People who have the preference to process information as **Construct** are the builders of the learning world. They have an uncanny ability to take new ideas and concepts and smash them together into something amazing and beautiful. This means a lot of hard work and practice, though, which is meant to help generate new, exciting theories and ideas. **Constructors** are the workhorse of the PP table, and for that reason, often thrive in competitive settings.

KEY ATTRIBUTES - CONSTRUCT
Want to practice and do something
Actively use new concepts

Construct learners like to do stuff. They like to learn by digging in and getting their hands dirty. You will find that they are happy any time they can build their knowledge base in real-world, practical ways. **Constructors**, too, often do a great job of blending the creativity needed to make large projects come together in a logical way with a deep-rooted base of inherent knowledge and information. For this reason, this is a particularly powerful PP for those in a leadership position.

HOW CAN I UNLOCK MY INNER GENIUS PROCESSING POWER – CONSTRUCT

Start today! When you are learning something new, we can **tailor our learning regimen to the mode of transmission. But, r**egardless of your Brain Fuel, once you've received the new information, it's time for processing. So, use these methods to Unlock your Inner Genius by transforming the information into something that works for you!

UNLOCK YOUR INNER GENIUS
Read given material
Hands-on activities
Test theories
Worksheets
Fact games
Puzzles
Drill

FAMOUS PEOPLE IN THE CLASS OF CONSTRUCT

Cristiano Ronaldo
Jack Welch
Megan Rapinoe
Michael Jordan
Prince Charles
Rihanna
Steve Jobs
Tory Burch

SHORT-CUT KEYS THAT YOU CAN USE TODAY TO UNLOCK YOUR INNER GENIUS

The following table is a **short-cut of tasks** that you can use to Unlock your Inner Genius and power your own learning. Keep this Fast-track Processing Power Lexicon at the ready. When processing new information, think about how you can extend your learning. As a **Construct PP,** think about how you can connect with other people to collaborate, have discussions, build meaning, share personal experiences and explore.

CONSTRUCT - FAST-TRACK PROCESSING POWER LEXICON
Applying new ideas
Building
Common sense
Creating usability
Executes or carries out the steps
Experimenting
Know what to do
Working application
Practice
Skills
Thinking and doing

THE IMPACT FOR YOU (ISN'T THAT IMPORTANT FOR YOU AS A CONSTRUCT PP?)

When you Unlock your Inner Genius and learn your Processing Power is in the **Construct** profile, you'll be able to tailor everything you do toward cultivating these considerations. You'll be able to relate your learning to your own experience and think about the benefit, the advantage, and the meaning of what you are learning. As you **tailor your learning regimen to the mode of transmission,** you will be able to use the methods to quickly take new information and put it into a process that works for you.

SUMMARY

- People who have the preference to process information as Construct have an uncanny ability to take new ideas and concepts and put them together into something useful.

- As a Construct PP, you are very likely going to successfully blend creativity with information.

- This Processing Power is ideally suited for those in leadership positions or aspiring to be in leadership positions.

UNLOCKING PEOPLE WHO HAVE 'CONSTRUCT PP'

As we have said before, knowing who you are, how you best process information is an excellent accelerator to **Unlocking your Inner Genius**. However, the real power is when you discover how to **Unlock the Inner Genius of others**. Let's discover how you can use your Inner Genius Keys to unlock the potential for people with the Construct Processing Power.

KEY QUESTION - CONSTRUCT

Is there one question that you can immediately tap into, expedite, and drive communication with those with the **Construct** Processing Power?

Imagine if there was one question that would **Construct** you to people that are not like you. Does that exist?

Luckily, yes. Ask this one **Key Question** to tap into and **Construct:**

How does it work?

You might also ask Constructors about how they might go about approaching a new puzzle or challenges. You could ask,

"What is your first instinct when you see a problem?"

Or,

"How do you begin to craft solutions?"

When you ask this Key Question, people who have a preference to process their information using Construct will often begin to provide magnificent insights. It will be like watching a rainstorm fall from the sky full of new ideas and information. They are building, and they will appreciate that opportunity. Remember, once you've asked this question, stop, listen and get ready to ask more questions to Connect.

PROCESSING POWER KEYS USED WHEN TEACHING OR PRESENTING

Given that people with the Construct Processing Power are all about making something new interaction, it makes sense that teaching, presenting, coaching, or communicating with them, their activities and methods (the keys) are about Constructing.

PROCESSING POWER KEYS – CONSTRUCT
Coaching
Consistency
Constant inquiry
Focus on applying information according to a specific situation
Discussion
Practice in a perfect world (i.e., what's been taught, without variation)

SHORT-CUT TASKS THAT YOU CAN USE TODAY

The following table is a short-cut of tasks that you can assign to attendees and participants to quickly key them in. Even without any pre-thought, you could do this on the fly.

Keep this Fast-track Processing Power Lexicon at the ready. This will help you to quickly assign a task with little preparation. For example, when you feel like your presentation needs some unlocking to key into people's profiles, refer to this Super List and quickly assign the group or individual a task. Too easy!

CONSTRUCT - FAST-TRACK PROCESSING POWER LEXICON
Applying new ideas
Building
Common sense
Creating usability
Executes or carries out the steps
Experimenting
Know what to do
Working application
Practice
Skills
Thinking and doing

KEY QUESTION CHECKLIST

After each time you present, train, coach, facilitate or converse, and just before you press 'send' on your next email, check to ensure that you have used your Construct PP Keys. Then, just before you finish, did you...?

DID I....
Provide the opportunity to practice?
Provide tools, templates, job aids to help?
Allocate all resources needed?
Coach along the way?

KEY WORDS TO SPRINKLE INTO YOUR LANGUAGE

When communicating with people who have the preference to process information as **Construct,** use building language. The benefit is that they'll feel like you are 'talking their language.'

WORDS TO COMMUNICATE WITH/TO THIS PROCESSING POWER

Accomplish	Achievement	Application
Apply	Assemble	Bring to fruition
Change	Commit	Complete
Conclude	Construct	Course of action
Create	Deliver on	Design
Develop	Discover	Dummy run
Enactment	Execution	Exercise
Experience	Fulfilment	Generate
Get done	Implement	Implementation
Interpret	Make	Make happen
Make it	Manufacture	Model
Negotiate	Organize	Perform
Pursuit	Prepare	Process
Produce	Put together	Putting into practice
Realize	Report	Run through
Solve	Try-out	Use
Utilization		

THE IMPACT FOR YOU - CONSTRUCT PP

It is always helpful to incorporate a diverse array of profiles whenever you are putting together a team or simply working on the day-to-day, collaborative activities. Constructors are excellent driving forces behind any project. They are critical to have when doing things like running a company or leading a team. Someone has to put it all together. The Construct PP individual is exactly who you should be looking for when making hiring selections or trying to edge out the competition.

SUMMARY

- Ask a **Construct PP:** *"How does it work?"* to prime their thinking and get them moving in the right direction.

- Constructors will likely be very comfortable when engaging in activities such as building, practicing, and trying out new things

- This PP is ideally suited for leadership roles, and you should keep this in mind as you make hiring and personnel decisions.

INVENT

PEOPLE WITH INVENT AS THEIR PROCESSING POWER: WHO ARE THEY?

People who have the preference to process information as **Inventors** share a lot of similarities to their Construct counterparts, except they are often the pinnacle of creative thinking. They are the experimenters of the PP table, and they are usually really good at coming up with new ideas based solely on their ability to try out and process so many variables and variations. It can be pretty fun to be in this class, as you will find lots of new ways of thinking and approaching concepts that others might not have considered.

KEY ATTRIBUTES – INVENT
Want to try out variations
Trying them out in life elsewhere
Identifying reasons to learn more

Invent learners excel when given a chance to figure things out independently and come up with answers by trial-and-error. They may initially reject the prescribed way of going about things as they will want a chance of their own to generate something better or more efficient. It is critical not to inhibit this process and let the **Inventor** have some leeway to play. By doing so, you are both facilitating their needed creative outlets and ensuring you do not frustrate them as learners. Both of these are essential things to keep in mind.

HOW CAN I UNLOCK MY INNER GENIUS PROCESSING POWER - INVENT

Start today! When you are learning something new we can **tailor our learning regimen to the mode of transmission.** Regardless of your Brain Fuel, once you've received the new information, it's time for processing. Use these methods to Unlock your Inner Genius by transforming the information into something that works for you!

UNLOCK YOUR INNER GENIUS
Tips, Tricks, Traps
Personal Action Plan
Group Action Plan
Write story or journal
Brainstorm uses in real life
Likely challenges in real life
Opportunities to change/modify process

FAMOUS PEOPLE IN THE CLASS OF INVENT

Bethenny Frankel
Coco Chanel
Elon Musk
Catherine Mattiske
Jacinda Ardern
Jameela Jamil
Oprah Winfrey
Pablo Picasso

SHORT-CUT KEYS THAT YOU CAN USE TODAY TO UNLOCK YOUR INNER GENIUS

The following table is a **short-cut of tasks** that you can use to Unlock your Inner Genius and power your own learning. Keep this Fast-track Processing Power Lexicon at the ready. When processing new information, think about how you can extend your learning. As an **Invent PP,** think about how you can connect with other people to collaborate, have discussions, build meaning, share personal experiences and explore.

INVENT - FAST-TRACK PROCESSING POWER LEXICON
Adaptation
Critical consideration
Doing
Dynamic
Ideation
Invention
Learn by trial and error
Seek hidden possibilities
Self-discovery
Tips, Tricks, Traps
Visioning

THE IMPACT FOR YOU

When you Unlock your Inner Genius and know that your Processing Power is **Invent** you'll be learning at an increased rate. Whatever you are learning will be less of a struggle. You'll be able to relate your learning to your own experience and think about the benefit, the advantage, and the meaning in what you are learning. As you **tailor your learning regimen to the mode of transmission,** you will be able to use the methods to quickly take new information and put it into a process that works for you.

SUMMARY

- People who have the preference to process information as Invent are the experimenters of the PP table.

- They often develop new ideas based on their ability to try out and process many variables and variations.

- Invent learners excel when given a chance to figure things out independently and come up with answers by trial-and-error.

UNLOCKING PEOPLE WHO HAVE 'INVENT' PP'

As we have said before, knowing who you are, how you best process information is a great accelerator to **Unlocking your Inner Genius**. However, the real power is when you discover how to **Unlock the Inner Genius of others**. Let's find out how you can use your Inner Genius Keys to unlock the potential for people with the **Invent** Processing Power.

KEY QUESTION - INVENT

Is there one question that you can use to immediately tap into, expedite and drive communication with those that have the **Invent** Processing Power?

Imagine if there was one question that would **Invent** you to people that are not like you. Does that exist?

Luckily, yes. Ask this one **Key Question** to tap into and **Invent:**

What are the possibilities?

This is a great question to ask anyone, really. A possibility is, basically, what this entire process is all about. However, it is conducive to ask this question, specifically, to the **Invent** learner. Other questions you might want to consider, as well, are:

"Where do we go from here?"

"How many different ways can we get where we want to go?"

When you ask this **Key Question**, people who have a preference to process their information using Invent will be jittery at the excitement of the possibilities you are presenting them with. These individuals love to think and fantasize about new options, and you will be giving them a chance to do just that. Remember, once you've asked this question, stop, listen and get ready to ask more questions to **Invent.**

PROCESSING POWER KEYS USED WHEN TEACHING OR PRESENTING

Given that people with the Invent Processing Power are all about finding meaning and building interaction, it makes sense that when you are teaching, presenting, coaching, or communicating with their activities and methods (the keys) are about Inventing.

PROCESSING POWER KEYS - INVENT
Creating interest and desire
Critical thinking
Diverse activities
Evaluating and making judgments based on information
Focus on parts and their functionality to the whole
Paint a vision for the future - what will the end result look like?
Practice with variation

Putting parts together in a new way
Questions that are not easily solved
Self-discovery
Surprises are opportunities

SHORT-CUT TASKS THAT YOU CAN USE TODAY

The following table is a **short-cut of tasks** that you can assign to attendees and participants to quickly key them in. Even without any pre-thought, you could do this on the fly.

Keep this Fast-track Processing Power Lexicon at the ready. This will help you to quickly assign a task with little preparation. When you feel like your presentation needs some unlocking to key into people's profile, refer to this Fast-track Processing Power Lexicon and quickly assign the group or individual a task. Too easy!

INVENT - FAST-TRACK PROCESSING POWER LEXICON
Adaptation
Critical consideration
Doing
Dynamic
Ideation
Invention
Learn by trial and error
Seek hidden possibilities
Self-discovery
Tips, Tricks, Traps
Visioning

KEY QUESTION CHECKLIST

After each time you present, train, coach, facilitate or converse, and just before you press 'send' on your next email, check to ensure that you have used your Invent PP Keys. Just before you finish, did you...?

DID I....
Celebrate progress?
Refine and adapt for real-world situations?
Provide tips, tricks, and shortcuts?
Provide traps that people might encounter?
Provide an opportunity to assess gaps?

KEY WORDS TO SPRINKLE INTO YOUR LANGUAGE

When communicating with people who have the preference to process information as **Invent,** use connecting language. The benefit is that they'll feel like you are 'talking their language.'

WORDS TO COMMUNICATE WITH/TO THIS PROCESSING POWER

Analyze	Appraise	Assess
Blue sky thinking	Brainstorm	Buzz session
Categorize	Classify	Combine
Compare	Conceptualize	Concocting
Consideration	Contrast	Convert
Creating	critical thinking	Criticize
Debate	Defend	Deliberate
Diagram	Differentiate	Disassemble
Dreaming up	Evolve	Examine
Exchange	Free thinking	Free-association
Group-think	Huddle	Hypothesize
Invent	Line of thought	Merge
Metamorphose	Problem solve	Reality check
Reason	Recommend	Research
Round table	Separate	Solve
Subdivide	Think	Transform
Value	Weigh	

THE IMPACT FOR YOU - INVENT

Inventors are the "lighting in a bottle" people we can all benefit from. They are the dreamers who come up with ideas and plans that can change the world. They must be allowed to explore these ideas and cultivate them. Too often, the Invent PP cuts down at the knees of other more rigid, less creative individuals. This is truly a shame. These people need space to grow and flourish. When they can, we all benefit.

SUMMARY

- Ask these individuals: *What are the possibilities? or* "Where do we go from here?"

- These individuals love to think and fantasize about new possibilities

- Give Inventors the space they need to experiment and grow; doing otherwise will stunt their ability to succeed.

STEP 3 – POWER-UPS: SUPER FUEL FOR YOUR INNER GENIUS

Congratulations! You've unlocked your Inner Genius by discovering your Brain Fuel and delving into your Processing Power. But, there is one last supercharge thing to realize: Power-Up.

When you know your unique Power-Up, you'll activate and energize your learning to stratospheric heights. Finding your Power-Up is like adding new power to your already amplified learning speed and ability to communicate to others.

Have you ever wondered why some people who have unremarkable jobs have a unique ability 'on the side'? Their career may not be utilizing their natural talent and leaving the essence of what they love to do and do best for times outside of work. Many people may be delighted with their 9 to 5 job and sing in the shower like an opera star. Their friends and family may remark that they should go on television shows like "America's Got Talent" or a similar show that causes all of us to shake our heads in disbelief of the performer's untapped talent.

All of us have a Power-Up.

*A Power-Up is a natural
intelligence that we have that,
when tapped, boosts our
connection to learning new
information.*

Your Power-Up gives you an exceptional or an extraordinary ability to speed up the amount of data you take in and process that information with ease. It's like the 'frosting on the cake' of your Inner Genius.

We all excel in different areas. When people can identify which Power-Up they use to learn, they can adapt the information to their learning preference.

While we initially focus on discovering your Power-Up, the benefit of you spotting other people's Power-Up is that you can communicate in an even more engaging way. This will expand the horizons for teachers, facilitators, learning professionals, parents, sports coaches, and anyone who is invested in the achievement of others.

The six Inner Genius Power-Ups are:

1. Independent

2. Collaborative

3. Linguistic

4. Number-Crunch

5. Classify

6. Rhythmic

Once you add your Power-Up to your Brain Fuel and Processing Power, you'll be learning and communicating with a new level of excellence. Your supremacy of learning new things at speed and quality of communication when sharing with others will be noticeable daily.

Let's explore each of the Power-Ups. To discover your unique Power-Up complete the Inner Genius Profile at:

www.innergeniusnow.com

INDEPENDENT POWER-UP

ABOUT YOUR POWER-UP: INDEPENDENT

You would prefer to be a soloist than in a chorus line. You excel under your own steam and enjoy autonomy. Pioneers represent the potential pinnacle of individual strength.

KEY ATTRIBUTES

The Independent has some strong attributes that drive their everyday life.

- Working alone can be just as effective as working in a group

- Engages in solo activities rather than team activities

- Likes hobbies that are solo (such as meditation, relaxing, photography, listening to podcasts, playing an instrument, writing, cooking, single-person athletic activity)

- Very happy being alone

- Reflects on themselves internally

- When working on a task, I prefer to get my own thoughts in order first before going to a team meeting

WORDS TO DESCRIBE THIS STYLE

- Tolerant of opposing viewpoints

- Not conforming to the ways or opinions of others

- Questioning spirit

- Not influenced by others

- Standing on their own

- Not dependent on others

- Working for oneself

- Decisions based on individual opinion or experience

- Not easily persuaded to change beliefs or opinions

- Able to function independently

- Able to provide for oneself

COMMUNICATING WITH THIS POWER-UP – INDEPENDENT

HOOK-IN QUESTION

Is there one question that will spark an Independent? Yes, try this at your next meeting, coaching session, parent to teenager talk.

*From what we are going to learn/have learned, **what resonates with you**?*

After you've asked it, stop and listen. Let them talk, and you might be amazed at what is revealed!

WORDS TO COMMUNICATE WITH/TO THIS POWER-UP

When you are working, coaching, teaching, talking or writing to people who have this Power-Up, sprinkle these words into your communication. These will 'hook in' your listener, reader, or learner, and as such, they'll feel a connection to you. With this rapport, they'll feel like they know, like, and trust you on a deeper level.

Assured	Autonomous	Bold
Broad-minded	Calm	Certain
Collected	Competent	Composed
Confident	Cool-headed	Courageous
Decisive	Determined	Distinct
Flexible	Free thought	Free-spirited
Freestanding	Freethinking	Freewheeling
Impartial	Individual	Individualistic
Maverick	Non-conformist	Open-minded
Originality	Perceptive	Poised
Positive	Purposeful	Radical
Revolutionary	Self-confident	Self-dependent
Self-direction	Self-reliant	Self-secure
Self-sufficient	Self-supporting	Self-subsistent
self-sustaining	Separate	Singular
Unaided	Unbounded	Uninhibited
Unorthodox	Unruffled	

HOOKS WHEN TEACHING OR PRESENTING

If you are a teacher, coach, manager, co-worker, parent, or someone who is imparting knowledge, try these 'hooks' to help accelerate their learning.

- Don't call on the first hand that goes up after you ask a question; pause and wait a moment for some of the introverts to catch up or to formulate their thoughts before volunteering.

- Gently invite Independent learners to add their thoughts after others have spoken.

- Provide opportunities for journaling, which enables engaging in introspection.

- Include periods of quiet and opportunities to experience solitude, such as in reflective journaling.

- Plan opportunities for independent learning.

- Provide physical space for "alone time" if possible.

- Invite Independent learners to analyze and reflect on material, such as case studies and stories, before sharing their thoughts.

- Encourage intrapersonal learners to use their imaginations to place themselves in stories from history.

- Invite Independent learners to reflect on and write down goals for what they hope to learn or achieve.

- Encourage exploration of historical interests, such as art museums.

- Encourage reading, especially before the learning program, to get a jump start on the learning.

- Gently but consistently encourage interaction with others.

- Invite students to take charge of tasks that require an organization that they can accomplish independently but for the benefit of others.

- Invite learners to express thoughts from the perspective of the content.

- Give intrapersonal learners time to think!

CHECK SHEET TO ENSURE THAT THE COMMUNICATION HOOKS INTO EACH TYPE

Did I....

- Create an opportunity to buy in?

- Provide an opportunity to reflect?

- Provide time to learn in individual activities?

- Balance information and practice time?

- Provide the opportunity to watch and listen?

COLLABORATIVE POWER-UP

ABOUT YOUR POWER-UP: COLLABORATIVE

You thrive in a group. You draw energy from connecting with people to share ideas, enjoy the company and evolve the world around you.

KEY ATTRIBUTES

If you have the Collaborative Power-Up, you have driving forces that charge up your day

- Let's try it out

- Achieves results with others

- Shares knowledge

- Shares ability

- Peer-to-peer networking

WORDS TO DESCRIBE THIS STYLE

- Sensing group feelings

- Harmonizing

- Compromising and encouraging

- Time-keeping

- Relieving tension

- Bringing people into a discussion

- Cooperative learner

- Mutual assistance in working towards a common goal

COMMUNICATING WITH THIS POWER-UP – COLLABORATIVE

HOOK-IN QUESTION

Is there one question that will spark the Collaborative? Yes, try this at your next meeting, coaching session, parent to teenager talk.

> *How could you **work with other people** to get you going /meet your goal / your problem solved?*

After you've asked this question focus your questions on 'who else' questions like"

> *Who else is involved?*
>
> *Who else can you talk to?*
>
> *Who else can help?*

WORDS TO COMMUNICATE WITH/TO THIS POWER-UP

When you are working, coaching, teaching, talking or writing to people who have this Power-Up, sprinkle these words into your communication. These will 'hook in' your listener, reader, or learner, and as such, they'll feel a connection to you. With this rapport, they'll feel like they know, like, and trust you on a deeper level.

Accommodating	Adaptable	Agreeing
Allied	Amenable	Assimilated
Coefficient	Collective	Combining
Combining	Communal	Community-based
Compliant	Composite	Concentrated
Concurring	Connected	Consolidated
Coordinated	Cumulative	Ensemble
Fused	Group	Groups
Hand in glove	Hand in hand	Harmonized
Helpful	In league	Interactive
Interdependent	Inter-professional	Joint
Linked	Multiple	Mutual
Obliging	Participating	Reciprocal
Responsive	Shared	Synergistic
Synergy	Team	Together
Two-way	Unified	Uniting
Willing		

HOOKS WHEN TEACHING OR PRESENTING

When you are working, coaching, teaching, talking or writing to people who have this Power-Up, sprinkle these words into your communication. These will 'hook in' your listener, reader, or learner, and as such, they'll feel a connection to you. With this rapport, they'll feel like they know, like, and trust you on a deeper level.

- Do something active with the information

- Establish group goals and objectives

- Build Trust

- Openly communicate

- Create Group Roles

- Active participation in learning or small group learning

- Not deprived of making contributions

- Teacher/trainer acts as the mediator

- Student-student communication

- Instructor-student communication

- Value diversity

- Willing to be of assistance

CHECK SHEET TO ENSURE THAT THE COMMUNICATION HOOKS INTO EACH TYPE

Did I...

- Check the other person's needs and mood?

- Provide the opportunity for collaboration and the ability to work in groups?

- When solving problems, ensure that they worked with others?

- Eliminate 'quiet' and ensure enough time to talk through problems/solutions/opinions?

- Provide feedback in a sensitive manner and preferably to a group rather than individually?

LINGUISTIC POWER-UP

ABOUT YOUR POWER-UP: LINGUISTIC

Whether a scribe or a songwriter, you use the art of language to craft and express your inner passions and prowess. Words and how you arrange them are your gift to those around you.

KEY ATTRIBUTES

The Linguistic Power-Up is fueled by the written word and spoken language.

Words are the propellent of their everyday life. They:

- Relate to language

- Are comfortable speaking in a group or public speaking

- May speak multiple languages and learns language with ease

WORDS TO DESCRIBE THIS STYLE

- Expresses and communicates via words

- Writes or produces literary work

- Actively engages in words and language

- Production of language

169

- Abstract reasoning

- Symbolic thinking

- Enjoys reading

- Confident in writing

COMMUNICATING WITH THIS POWER-UP – LINGUISTIC

HOOK-IN QUESTION

Is there one question that will spark a Linguistic? Yes, try this at your next meeting, coaching session, parent to teenager talk.

*Can you **describe in detail** the situation/problem/opportunity?*

WORDS TO COMMUNICATE WITH/TO THIS POWER-UP

When you are working, coaching, teaching, talking, or writing to people who have this Power-Up, sprinkle these words into your communication. These will 'hook in' your listener, reader, or learner, and as such, they'll feel a connection to you. With this rapport, they'll feel like they know, like, and trust you on a deeper level.

Author	Contributor	Creative writer
Editor	Expressive	Intellectual
Interpreter	Language	Linguist
Rhetorical	Scribe	Storytelling
Verbal	Well-informed	Word smart
Writer		

HOOKS WHEN TEACHING OR PRESENTING

When you are working, coaching, teaching, talking or writing to people who have this Power-Up, sprinkle these words into your communication. These will 'hook in' your listener, reader, or learner, and as such, they'll feel a connection to you. With this rapport, they'll feel like they know, like, and trust you on a deeper level.

- Teach-backs - get them to present key ideas or concepts to the class or group

- Use creative writing activities

- Set up debates

- Allow for formal speaking opportunities

- Provide plenty of reading opportunities

- Create a poem or story about key concepts/learning

- Playing word-based games (such as scrabble, crosswords, find a word, etc.)

- Listening to stories

- Listening to experts speak (e.g., TED Talks)

CHECK SHEET TO ENSURE THAT THE COMMUNICATION HOOKS INTO EACH TYPE

Did I...

- Take care with the words that I said?

- Listen carefully to their words?

- Allow the person to explain in detail their point of view/opinion?

- Give reading and writing opportunities rather than just relying on the spoken word?

- Model their love of language?

NUMBER-CRUNCH POWER-UP

ABOUT YOUR POWER-UP: NUMBER-CRUNCH

In the equation 'the whole is greater than the sum of its parts,' you are the sum. This is because you are analytical and considered and hold the world around you to account.

KEY ATTRIBUTES

The Number-Crunch Power-Up is the mathematical worker who analyses facts, data, and information. Numbers fuel their lives. They are great when:

- Performing complex math or arithmetic

- Resembling mathematics in being rigorously precise

WORDS TO DESCRIBE THIS STYLE

- Works well in all fields of mathematics

- Skilled in analytics

- A numerical analyst

- Enjoys computation and is a statistics theoretician

COMMUNICATING WITH THIS POWER-UP – NUMBER-CRUNCH

Often those with the Number-Crunch Power-Up might be hesitant to delve into their souls to uncover their feelings. Being facts and data-fuelled folks, it might take a couple of questions for the Number Crunch Power-Up to relate what they are going through now. Try this line of questions next time you need to get deep into conversation with your Number-Cruncher friend, colleague, direct report, coachee, or family member:

Tell me about a time when you were able to develop a different-problem solving approach.

How could that relate to what you are working on/ going through now?

WORDS TO COMMUNICATE WITH/TO THIS POWER-UP

When you are working, coaching, teaching, talking or writing to people who have this Power-Up, sprinkle these words into your communication. These will 'hook in' your listener, reader, or learner, and as such, they'll feel a connection to you. With this rapport, they'll feel like they know, like, and trust you on a deeper level.

Accurate	Analyst	Analytical
Arithmetic	Attentive	Authority
Boffin	Calculator	Careful
Clear	Computing	Conscientious
Correct	Counting	Detailed
Diligent	Estimation	Exact
Exacting	Expert	Fastidious
Figures	Finicky	Forecaster
Logical	Measured	Methodical
Meticulous	Nuanced	Numbers
Objective	Ordered	Organized

Perfectionist	Persnickety	Pinpoint
Precise	Proper	Regulated
Savant	Specialist	Spot-on
Statistics	Strict	Studious
Systematic	Thorough	Totalizer
Ultra-careful	Well-organized	

HOOKS WHEN TEACHING OR PRESENTING

When you are working, coaching, teaching, talking or writing to people who have this Power-Up, sprinkle these words into your communication. These will 'hook in' your listener, reader, or learner, and as such, they'll feel a connection to you. With this rapport, they'll feel like they know, like, and trust you on a deeper level.

- Playing math games like mancala, dominoes, chess, checkers, and Monopoly

- Searching for patterns in the classroom, school, outdoors, and home

- Conducting experiments to demonstrate science concepts

- Using science tool kits for science programs

- Creating clear step-by-step directions

- Providing facts and data before asking them to practice

- Designing alphabetic and numeric codes

CHECK SHEET TO ENSURE THAT THE COMMUNICATION HOOKS INTO EACH TYPE

Did I...

- Provide opportunities to discuss logic?

- Did the person figure things out and come up with unusual solutions?

- Explain the data/steps/process clearly?

- Have a stepwise plan for execution?

- Equip people with all knowledge and information needed?

CLASSIFY POWER-UP

ABOUT YOUR POWER-UP: CLASSIFY

"A place for everything and everything in its place." You like order and structure. Things can be fun or unexpected, but they need to be sensible and sorted.

KEY ATTRIBUTES

The Classify Power-Up is super-charged by organization, categorization, and sorting. They find relationships between the most disparate things, making connections between random ideas to create and invent genius new ideas. They:

- Assign to a particular class or category

- Arrange things in order

- Characterize people/things by listing their qualities

- Make descriptions within a narrative

- Enjoy nature and the outdoors

WORDS TO DESCRIBE THIS STYLE

- Separates the wheat from the chaff

- Makes a distinction between one thing and another

- A class, group, or kind sharing specific characteristics or qualities

COMMUNICATING WITH THIS POWER-UP – CLASSIFY

HOOK-IN QUESTION

What are a couple of questions you can rely on when trying to spark someone with the Classify Power-Up? Then, try these ones at your next meeting, coaching session, parent to teenager talk.

What's a way that you can take what you are doing now and put it into a new order that makes sense?

How can you take this apart and analyze each part? And, then, how can you put it together in a new way?

WORDS TO COMMUNICATE WITH/TO THIS POWER-UP

When you are working, coaching, teaching, talking or writing to people who have this Power-Up, sprinkle these words into your communication. These will 'hook in' your listener, reader, or learner, and as such, they'll feel a connection to you. With this rapport, they'll feel like they know, like, and trust you on a deeper level.

Arrange	Array	Ascertain
Assign	Assortment	Badge
Brand	Catalog	Character
Codify	Compartmentalize	Depict
Describe	Distinguish	Divide up
Draw up	Feature	Group
Hallmark	Hold a candle to	Identification

Identify	Individualize	Marshal
Methodize	Model	Name
Nominate	Organize	Outline
Personify	Put in order	Quality
Quirk	Rank	Rate
Regulate	Select	Sift out
Soul	Stack up against	Symbolize
Systematize	Tell apart	Tell between
Tell from	Triage	Weed out

HOOKS WHEN TEACHING OR PRESENTING

When you are working, coaching, teaching, talking or writing to people who have this Power-Up, sprinkle these words into your communication. These will 'hook in' your listener, reader, or learner, and as such, they'll feel a connection to you. With this rapport, they'll feel like they know, like, and trust you on a deeper level.

- Have in-depth discussions outdoors, in nature

- Create activities that are based on finding patterns

- Review disjoined materials with a challenge to find the relationships between the parts

- Create case studies without an ending. Assign the task of finishing off the case study by using reference materials to form an argument and solution

- Challenge working systems to be reworked to find improvements

- Put steps in order

- Classify tasks, objects, or processes into categories

- Set identification activities, like scavenger hunts whereby methodical strategies a solution is found

- Ranking activities, like polling, where opinions are sought and then presented back as a summary

CHECK SHEET TO ENSURE THAT THE COMMUNICATION HOOKS INTO EACH TYPE

Did I...

- Provide opportunities to interact with nature?

- Spend time working on patterns and relationships?

- Set tasks that included classification and categorization?

- Have discussions in the outdoors?

- Provide opportunities to explore solutions to problems using systems?

RHYTHMIC POWER-UP

ABOUT YOUR POWER-UP: RHYTHMIC

You have a toe-tapping tempo about you. You like to get moving and keep moving. Things make sense to you when they have a rhythmic flow or sequence to them

KEY ATTRIBUTES

The Rhythmic Power-Up is the heart-beat of the group who is never far from music, be it listening, playing, or composing. Their life's fuel is the rhythm of the world around them. They are notable for:

- Having or relating to rhythm

- Responding to regular, repetitive motion or sound

- Being smoothly elegant or graceful in movement

- Relating to music

- Relating to poetry and rhyme

HOOKS WHEN TEACHING OR PRESENTING

- Creating music videos

- Writing poetry and pop songwriting

WORDS TO DESCRIBE THIS STYLE

- Expresses themselves via music and beat

- Writes rhythmically with sentences that are well structured

- Actively engages with music, from morning to night

- Concentrates better with music around them, or conversely finds it a complete distraction (either end of the spectrum)

- Enjoys listening to music

- May play a musical instrument or composes music

- Often has a song playing in their mind

COMMUNICATING WITH THIS POWER-UP – RHYTHMIC

Is there one question that will spark a Rythmic? Yes, try this at your next meeting, coaching session, parent to teenager talk.

What sounds best to you?

WORDS TO COMMUNICATE WITH/TO THIS POWER-UP

When you are working, coaching, teaching, talking, or writing to people who have this Power-Up, sprinkle these words into your communication. These will 'hook in' your listener, reader, or learner, and as such, they'll feel a connection to you. With this rapport, they'll feel like they know, like, and trust you on a deeper level.

Agile	Agreeable	Cadenced
Constant	Cyclical	Deft
Dramatic	Driving	Effortless
Elegant	Emotional	Enthusiastic
Expressive	Figurative	Flowing
Fluid	Funky	Graceful
Gracious	Harmonic	Imaginative
Impassioned	Inspired	Jazzy
Lyrical	Measured	Melodious
Metrical	Musical	Nimble
Occasional	Passionate	Perpetual
Personal	Pleasing	Poetic
Recurring	Rhythmical	Sentimental
Smooth	Steady	Sweet-sounding
Uplifting	Whimsical	

HOOKS WHEN TEACHING OR PRESENTING

When you are working, coaching, teaching, talking or writing to people who have this Power-Up, sprinkle these words into your communication. These will 'hook in' your listener, reader, or learner, and as such, they'll feel a connection to you. With this rapport, they'll feel like they know, like, and trust you on a deeper level.

- Create music videos to summarize key learning points

- Play music before the class or presentation, during activities, and on breaks

- Write poetry or a song to put critical concepts to music

- Associate new ideas with music. Allocate a theme song to a new team or group initiative

- Create Listening Bingo where each bingo square is a sound that relates to a critical point, a step of a process, or a concept

- Create a competition for the best poem, rap, rhythm, or rhyme to review the new learning or concept

- Reword the steps of a business process, step-by-step process, or list of instructions into word patterns, musical mnemonics, rhythmic language

CHECK SHEET TO ENSURE THAT THE COMMUNICATION HOOKS INTO EACH TYPE

Did I...

- Include music, rhythm, and or environmental sounds?

- Explore their feelings about a particular piece of music?

- Explain concepts by allowing them to create rhythms, raps, or rhymes?

- Give them time to put new information into a rhyme or beat?

- Play different styles of music throughout the day?

PART 5.
YOUR INNER GENIUS ARCHETYPE

Now that you have explored Brain Fuel, Processing Power, and Power-Ups, you're ready to discover the intricacies of your Inner Genius Archetype.

Your Inner Genius Archetype is your unique combination of how you learn and process new information. When you add your Power-Up to your Inner Genius Archetype, you're unstoppable in your abilities to take up new information in a way that works for you, then synthesize and process that information for maximum efficiency.

Also, we can turn our attention to other people around us. How do you more effectively work, parent, manage, coach, train, teach or be a friend to an Archetype different from yours?

In this Part of Unlock Inner Genius, we'll explore your unique Inner Genius Archetype so that you can power your path to extraordinary success – both by knowing your own Archetype and being able to confidently work with other Archetypes!

Your Inner Genius Archetype can become a short-cut language to help you communicate with the world and for others communicate to you. For example, "I'm a Mason – talk to me about practical hands-on stuff," or "I'm a Futurist – I'm interested in change, challenge, tips, tricks and traps," or "I'm a Narrator – I'm energized by discussing how this connects to others."

During times of learning struggle, your Archetype becomes a motivator. You might be having difficulties learning something new. Leaning on your Archetype gives your strength. For example, "I am not understanding this yet, but I am a Decrypter so I need to draw and look at the how this connects to me and my world around me. I may be having difficulty right now but I'm a Decrypter and that's my power!"

There are 12 Inner Genius Archetypes. To unlock yours, complete the Inner Genius Profile at:

www.innergeniusnow.com

INNER GENIUS ARCHETYPE MATRIX

The Inner Genius Archetype Matrix plots the profile results of Brain Fuel and Processing Power. The intersection of Brain Fuel and Processing Power denotes a person's Inner Genius Archetype.

		PROCESSING POWER			
		CONNECT	DETAIL	CONSTRUCT	INVENT
BRAIN FUEL PROFILE	VISUAL	THE DECRYPTER	THE SCRIBE	THE CARTOGRAPHER	THE FUTURIST
	AUDITORY	THE NARRATOR	THE VALEDICTORIAN	THE COMPOSER	THE ENERGIZER
	KINESTHETIC	THE CATALYST	THE HOROLOGIST	THE MASON	THE EXPLORER

Figure 1 - Inner Genius Archetype Matrix

There are 12 Inner Genius Archetypes. To unlock yours, complete the Inner Genius Profile at:

www.innergeniusnow.com

THE DECRYPTER

YOUR INNER GENIUS ARCHETYPE

		PROCESSING POWER			
		CONNECT	DETAIL	CONSTRUCT	INVENT
BRAIN FUEL PROFILE	VISUAL	THE DECRYPTER	THE SCRIBE	THE CARTOGRAPHER	THE FUTURIST
	AUDITORY	THE NARRATOR	THE VALEDICTORIAN	THE COMPOSER	THE ENERGIZER
	KINESTHETIC	THE CATALYST	THE HOROLOGIST	THE MASON	THE EXPLORER

HOW THE WORLD SEES THE DECRYPTER

With a keen eye for the big picture and the inquisition to make connections, Decryter's seek clues to piece together understanding.

They uncover information and then piece it together to find patterns, gain insight, elevate relevance and find opportunities. They find relationships between seemingly unrelated ideas that are invisible to others.

THE DECRYPTER - WHAT YOUR SYMBOL MEANS

The Decrypter symbol combines two elements of the eye and keyhole.

The eye gives the idea of visualization and perspective that people sometimes only rarely see, and sometimes what The Decrypter sees is not apparent to others. The Decrypter knows the power of connection through responsibility, perception, and cognition. They have a heightened knowledge or a perception of others around them.

The keyhole is the key to connect and find ideas from visualization of thoughts that other people often don't see. The Decrypter effortlessly unlocks opportunities for business, personal, or family success by connecting through relationships.

The Decrypter shows their Inner Genius by always thinking and looking for meaning, asking 'why' from unusual perspectives to solve problems or find connections and solutions.

HOW DECRYPTERS RECEIVE NEW INFORMATION

The world is your canvas. If a picture tells a thousand words, you'll take the picture every time. Your brain fuel is a color-coded menu of symbols and maps. You see patterns and talk in pictures.

WORDS TO DESCRIBE THE DECRYPTER

- Humanize

- Feeling

- Personal Experience

- Asking Why?

FAMOUS DECRYPTERS

- Bill Gates

- Malala Yousafzai

HOW TO UNLOCK YOUR INNER GENIUS - DECRYPTER

WAYS YOU HOOK INTO NEW INFORMATION - YOUR SWEET SPOT

You use your strong understanding of 'why' to paint a unique picture of a situation.

KEY LEARNING ATTRIBUTES

- Want to know the reason for learning

- Identify a reason to learn

- Find a reason to engage with the topic

- Focus on past and present understanding

- Recognize current knowledge and engage for more learning

- Contribute to individual's perspective

HOW CAN YOU TAP INTO YOUR DECRYPTER GENIUS ZONE?

Map ideas and information into diagrams and color patterns.

HARNESS YOUR GLOBAL LEARNING PREFERENCE

- Prefer learning by observing the bigger picture

- Are holistic

- Learn in large chunks

- Absorb materials almost randomly without seeing connections, then suddenly 'get it.'

- Solve complex problems quickly

- Once they've grasped the big picture can put things together in novel ways but may not explain how they did it

- Have strong sequential abilities AFTER they've grasped the big picture

WAYS TO TURBO-LEARN IN YOUR INNER GENIUS ZONE

No matter how the information is coming to you, power your learning to turbo by:

- Ask WII-FM questions

191

- Demonstrate new learning to others

- Create a Mind map

- Brainstorm

- Make a logo

- Turn the information into an Image

- Discuss meaning and relevance with others

THE NARRATOR

YOUR INNER GENIUS ARCHETYPE

		PROCESSING POWER			
		CONNECT	DETAIL	CONSTRUCT	INVENT
BRAIN FUEL PROFILE	VISUAL	THE DECRYPTER	THE SCRIBE	THE CARTOGRAPHER	THE FUTURIST
	AUDITORY	THE NARRATOR	THE VALEDICTORIAN	THE COMPOSER	THE ENERGIZER
	KINESTHETIC	THE CATALYST	THE HOROLOGIST	THE MASON	THE EXPLORER

HOW THE WORLD SEES THE NARRATOR

The heart of a story is how Narrators connect with their world. The lyrical nature of a tale sets the stage for Narrators to converse with their audience.

They engage in discussions on the benefits, advantages, and relevance and how it relates to the overall goal.

THE NARRATOR - WHAT YOUR SYMBOL MEANS

The Narrator's symbol is the Owl, born from the tradition of the Owl being representative of a Guru since ancient times, which symbolizes a wise, intelligent animal, the center of all knowledge. The owl represents wisdom and vision. The Narrator harnesses the ability to explain connections that others miss. They help us understand the world around us and have inner knowledge of why things happen the way they do.

The owl is encased in the circle icon to represent an ecosystem where the audience's attraction is naturally enlightened by The Narrator. The circle symbolizes the cycle of time and represents completeness and equality. The Narrator engages with people by being equality-driven with the generosity of sharing and connecting to the world around them.

The Narrator takes intentional time to ponder, gain added meaning and values the future of friends, family, and co-workers. The Narrator shares wisdom for anyone willing to receive new knowledge in their 'circle.' People with open minds who stop to listen will be enlightened by The Narrator.

194

HOW NARRATORS RECEIVE NEW INFORMATION

Your life has a soundtrack. You connect to your world through sound and rhythm, the spoken word, and listening to and collaborating with experts. Your brain fuel takes things off the page and communicates them via the airwaves.

WORDS TO DESCRIBE THE NARRATOR

- Meaning

- Personify

- Trust

- Why?

FAMOUS NARRATORS

- Martin Luther King

- Mahatma Gandhi

HOW TO UNLOCK YOUR INNER GENIUS

WAYS YOU HOOK INTO NEW INFORMATION - YOUR SWEET SPOT

You love a workshop! Get all the ideas out on the table. Understand a range of perspectives.

KEY LEARNING ATTRIBUTES

- Want to know the reason for learning

- Identify a cause to learn

- Find a reason to engage with the topic

- Focus on past and present understanding

- Recognize current knowledge and engage in more learning

- Contribute to individual's perspective

HOW CAN YOU TAP INTO YOUR NARRATOR GENIUS ZONE

You love a good story. Actively look for podcasts or interviews with inspiring people who align with your goals.

HARNESS YOUR GLOBAL LEARNING PREFERENCE

- Prefer learning by observing the bigger picture

- Are holistic

- Learn in large chunks

- Absorb materials almost randomly without seeing connections, then suddenly 'get it'

- Solve complex problems quickly

- Once they've grasped the big picture can put things together in novel ways but may not explain how they did it

- Have strong sequential abilities AFTER they've grasped the big picture

WAYS TO TURBO-LEARN IN YOUR INNER GENIUS ZONE

No matter how the information is coming to you, power your learning to turbo by:

- Ask WII-FM questions

- Demonstrate new learning to others

- Create a Mind map

- Brainstorm

- Make a logo

- Turn the information into an Image

- Discuss meaning and relevance with others

THE CATALYST

YOUR INNER GENIUS ARCHETYPE

		PROCESSING POWER			
		CONNECT	DETAIL	CONSTRUCT	INVENT
BRAIN FUEL PROFILE	VISUAL	THE DECRYPTER	THE SCRIBE	THE CARTOGRAPHER	THE FUTURIST
	AUDITORY	THE NARRATOR	THE VALEDICTORIAN	THE COMPOSER	THE ENERGIZER
	KINESTHETIC	THE CATALYST	THE HOROLOGIST	THE MASON	THE EXPLORER

HOW THE WORLD SEES THE CATALYST

Catalysts facilitate change. Through active participation, clear instruction and hands on collaboration, Catalysts give individuals purpose and inspire them to bring their A game. In doing so they break down barriers and create common goals which move companies, classes and communities forward.

THE CATALYST - WHAT YOUR SYMBOL MEANS

The Catalyst symbol is built on the idea of the infinite symbol. The endless, infinite symbol provides the opportunity to form a recycling ecosystem that renews outdated thinking into fresh thinking.

Catalysts can think openly and combine, collaborate and form an ecosystem (companies, groups, classes) because the ecosystem has already been created. Then all difficulties or obstacles can be passed with enthusiasm by the group itself and make the team's strength unlimited.

In the center of The Catalyst symbol is a circle. Unlimited power is represented by the circle symbol, which represents the core of the whole of each individual who becomes one ecosystem, "The Catalyst." Here we represent Catalysts who drive the power of the collective.

The Catalyst is an ecosystem that facilitates and brings together each individual through collaboration that forms groups, classes, companies and makes the team with unlimited strength that can dispel difficulties and obstacles.

HOW CATALYSTS RECEIVE NEW INFORMATION

HANDS UP? HANDS DOWN? JUST MAKE SURE IT'S HANDS-ON! GET IN, GET STARTED, GET ON WITH IT. YOUR BRAIN FUEL IS A MOVING FEAST OF TACTILE ACTIVITY.

WORDS TO DESCRIBE THE CATALYSTS

- Collaboration

- Feeling

- Personal Incentive

- WII-FM

FAMOUS CATALYSTS

- Sigmund Freud

- Stephen Hawking

HOW TO UNLOCK YOUR INNER GENIUS

WAYS YOU HOOK INTO NEW INFORMATION - YOUR SWEET SPOT

Nothing ventured, nothing gained. You gain knowledge from getting involved. Trial and error are better than no trial at all.

KEY LEARNING ATTRIBUTES

- Want to know the reason for learning

- Identify a reason to learn

- Find a reason to engage with the topic

- Focus on past and present understanding

- Recognize current knowledge and engage in more learning

- Contribute to individual's perspective

HOW CAN YOU TAP INTO YOUR CATALYST GENIUS ZONE

*Go to the source of information.
Literally visit, touch, experience it
as much as possible.*

HARNESS YOUR GLOBAL LEARNING PREFERENCE

- Prefer learning by observing the bigger picture

- Are holistic

- Learn in large chunks

- Absorb materials almost randomly without seeing connections, then suddenly 'get it.'

- Solve complex problems quickly

- Once they've grasped the big picture can put things together in novel ways but may not explain how they did it

- Have strong sequential abilities AFTER they've grasped the big picture

201

WAYS TO TURBO-LEARN IN YOUR INNER GENIUS ZONE

No matter how the information is coming to you, power your learning to turbo by:

- Ask WII-FM questions

- Demonstrate new learning to others

- Create a Mind map

- Brainstorm

- Make a logo

- Turn the information into an Image

- Discuss meaning and relevance with others

THE SCRIBE

YOUR INNER GENIUS ARCHETYPE

		PROCESSING POWER			
BRAIN FUEL PROFILE		**CONNECT**	**DETAIL**	**CONSTRUCT**	**INVENT**
	VISUAL	THE DECRYPTER	THE SCRIBE	THE CARTOGRAPHER	THE FUTURIST
	AUDITORY	THE NARRATOR	THE VALEDICTORIAN	THE COMPOSER	THE ENERGIZER
	KINESTHETIC	THE CATALYST	THE HOROLOGIST	THE MASON	THE EXPLORER

HOW THE WORLD SEES THE SCRIBE

Chapter and verse, Scribes capture all the details from beginning to end. They diligently formulate the particulars and capture them in visual ways as a reference for others.

THE SCRIBE - WHAT YOUR SYMBOL MEANS

The Scribe symbol combines the quill and paper icon. Where a quill and paper are symbols of history or the beginning of ancient tools used by scribes. Without The Scribes, there would be no journal of how this civilization developed. Through The Scribe, we can look for references to people's history and their problems. Finally, The Scribe's journals find solutions through detailed visual works.

The quill of the Scribe has a nib that is sharp with detail and inspires others with the flight of fancy plumed feather. Their unmatched brilliance has excellent flexibility to write, draw and illustrate their ideas with precision details like an ancient manuscript.

The Scribe is a journalist, a wise illuminator who becomes a reference for others without expecting anything in return. Scribes help every individual and community know more about the history and the purpose of the journey.

HOW SCRIBES RECEIVE NEW INFORMATION

The world is your canvas. If a picture tells a thousand words, you'll take the picture every time. Your brain fuel is a color-coded menu of symbols and maps. You see patterns and talk in pictures.

WORDS TO DESCRIBE THE SCRIBE

- Concepts

- Detail

- Facts

- Statistics

FAMOUS SCRIBES

- J K Rowling

- Jane Austin

HOW TO UNLOCK YOUR INNER GENIUS - SCRIBE

WAYS YOU HOOK INTO NEW INFORMATION - YOUR SWEET SPOT

You inherently map intangible concepts with tangible facts and align them with a structure that makes sense.

KEY LEARNING ATTRIBUTES

- Want to get the facts and concepts

- Formulate concepts about the topic

- Congruent structures and processes

HOW CAN YOU TAP INTO YOUR SCRIBE GENIUS ZONE

Gather information into color-coded zones and lists.

HARNESS YOUR SPECIFIC LEARNING PREFERENCE

- Sequential Learners

- Logical & Stepwise

- Prefer presentation in a linear and orderly manner

- Instructions in steps

- Learn in linear steps

- Each step follows logically from the last one

- Follow a logical stepwise approach to finding solutions

- Know the specific aspects of the subject but may have difficulty relating them to different subjects

- If a presenter jumps around and skips steps, you may have trouble following.

WAYS TO TURBO-LEARN IN YOUR INNER GENIUS ZONE

No matter how the information is coming to you, power your learning to turbo by:

- Lecture

- Timelines

- Charts, graphs

- Example of the finished product

- Step-by-step processes

- Flowcharts

- Pictures

THE VALEDICTORIAN

YOUR INNER GENIUS ARCHETYPE

		PROCESSING POWER			
		CONNECT	DETAIL	CONSTRUCT	INVENT
BRAIN FUEL PROFILE	VISUAL	THE DECRYPTER	THE SCRIBE	THE CARTOGRAPHER	THE FUTURIST
	AUDITORY	THE NARRATOR	THE VALEDICTORIAN	THE COMPOSER	THE ENERGIZER
	KINESTHETIC	THE CATALYST	THE HOROLOGIST	THE MASON	THE EXPLORER

HOW THE WORLD SEES THE VALEDICTORIAN

Valedictorians are consummate learners. Through listening and discussion, they deeply understand the essence of any situation and easily translate how small details contribute to the bigger picture.

THE VALEDICTORIAN - WHAT YOUR SYMBOL MEANS

The Valedictorian symbol using two elements. The main element is a book, plus a door that forms a building or house.

The book icon represents a source of learning knowledge that is always held by The Valedictorian. Valedictorians think rationally. They're able to listen and speak based on facts, create open places. This is represented by the symbol of the house, to shelter and listen to all kinds of discussions. They can see the point of view of problems that are rarely seen by people other.

The Valedictorian is an avid learner. They can judge things from multiple points of view and be a home for any discussion. Thus, being a good listener, understanding the essence of any situation deeply, and quickly translating how small details contribute to the bigger picture is the proclamation of the Valedictorian that they contribute to the world.

HOW VALEDICTORIANS RECEIVE NEW INFORMATION

Your life has a soundtrack. You connect to your world through sound and rhythm, the spoken word, and listening to and collaborating with experts. Your brain fuel takes things off the page and communicates them via the airwaves.

WORDS TO DESCRIBE THE VALEDICTORIAN

- Analytical
- Learning what experts think
- Data
- Thinking

FAMOUS VALEDICTORIANS

- Amanda Gorman
- Nicola Sturgeon

HOW TO UNLOCK YOUR INNER GENIUS - VALEDICTORIAN

WAYS YOU HOOK INTO NEW INFORMATION - YOUR SWEET SPOT

You like to read through instructions as a group where possible. It helps you better understand and implement them.

KEY LEARNING ATTRIBUTES

- Want to get the facts and concepts

- Formulate concepts about the topic

- Congruent structures and processes

HOW CAN YOU TAP INTO YOUR VALEDICTORIAN GENIUS ZONE

*Make up a catchy rhyme or routine
to help you keep something top of
mind.*

HARNESS YOUR SPECIFIC LEARNING PREFERENCE

- Sequential Learners

- Logical & Stepwise

- Prefer presentation in a linear and orderly manner

- Instructions in steps

- Learn in linear steps

- Each step follows logically from the last one

- Follow logical stepwise approach to finding solutions

- Know the specific aspects of the subject but may have difficulty relating them to different subjects

- If a presenter jumps around and skips steps, you may have trouble following.

WAYS TO TURBO-LEARN IN YOUR INNER GENIUS ZONE

No matter how the information is coming to you, power your learning to turbo by:

- Lecture

- Timelines

- Charts, graphs

- Example of the finished product

- Step-by-step processes

- Flowcharts

- Pictures

THE HOROLOGIST

YOUR INNER GENIUS ARCHETYPE

		PROCESSING POWER			
		CONNECT	DETAIL	CONSTRUCT	INVENT
BRAIN FUEL PROFILE	VISUAL	THE DECRYPTER	THE SCRIBE	THE CARTOGRAPHER	THE FUTURIST
	AUDITORY	THE NARRATOR	THE VALEDICTORIAN	THE COMPOSER	THE ENERGIZER
	KINESTHETIC	THE CATALYST	THE HOROLOGIST	THE MASON	THE EXPLORER

HOW THE WORLD SEES THE HOROLOGIST

This specialist technician is determined to ensure all the miniature cogs are in pristine working order so that the world around it can operate punctually.

THE HOROLOGIST - WHAT YOUR SYMBOL MEANS

The symbol of The Horologist combines the gear, clock, moon, and sun icons. Symbolized by the moon and sun icons, these are the icons of driving systems from the world around The Horologist.

The Horologist is practical and focused and moves with precision symbolized by the gear icon. It illustrates the connection between short-term repetition and how it contributes to long-term solutions. The gear icon also represents The Horologist's ability to be part of a greater whole and the critical and importance of their role.

In the center of the symbol is the clock icon. The traditional role of The Horologist being the clockmaker and technician adds a level of efficiency. The Horologist is a specialist who moves the center of the world order around them to maintain balance very efficiently. The clock is set to lucky number nine. In Chinese culture, the clock showing the number nine tells us Horologists are auspicious and able to create an easy and relaxed atmosphere endowed with the gift to serve others.

HOW HOROLOGISTS RECEIVE NEW INFORMATION

Hands up? Hands down? Just make sure it's hands-on! Get in, get started, get on with it. Your brain fuel is a moving feast of tactile activity.

WORDS TO DESCRIBE THE HOROLOGIST

- Formulating ideas
- Processes
- Step-by-step
- Logical Flow

FAMOUS HOROLOGISTS

- Serena Williams
- Warren Buffet

HOW TO UNLOCK YOUR INNER GENIUS - HOROLOGIST

WAYS YOU HOOK INTO NEW INFORMATION - YOUR SWEET SPOT

You are a tactile technician. You are keen to participate with a hands-on approach.

KEY LEARNING ATTRIBUTES

- Want to get the facts and concepts

- Formulate concepts about the topic

- Congruent structures and processes

HOW CAN YOU TAP INTO YOUR HOROLOGIST GENIUS ZONE

Experience is key in how you gather, process, and share information. Sharing information from others builds insight too.

HARNESS YOUR SPECIFIC LEARNING PREFERENCE

- Sequential Learners

- Logical & Stepwise

- Prefer presentation in a linear and orderly manner

- Instructions in steps

- Learn in linear steps

- Each step follows logically from the last one

- Follow stepwise analytical approach to finding solutions

- Know the specific aspects of the subject but may have difficulty relating them to different subjects

- If a presenter jumps around and skips steps, you may have trouble following.

WAYS TO TURBO-LEARN IN YOUR INNER GENIUS ZONE

No matter how the information is coming to you, power your learning to turbo by:

- Lecture

- Timelines

- Charts, graphs

- Example of the finished product

- Step-by-step processes

- Flowcharts

- Pictures

THE CARTOGRAPHER

YOUR INNER GENIUS ARCHETYPE

		PROCESSING POWER			
		CONNECT	**DETAIL**	**CONSTRUCT**	**INVENT**
BRAIN FUEL PROFILE	**VISUAL**	THE DECRYPTER	THE SCRIBE	THE CARTOGRAPHER	THE FUTURIST
	AUDITORY	THE NARRATOR	THE VALEDICTORIAN	THE COMPOSER	THE ENERGIZER
	KINESTHETIC	THE CATALYST	THE HOROLOGIST	THE MASON	THE EXPLORER

HOW THE WORLD SEES THE CARTOGRAPHER

With their innate ability to think in pictures, Cartographers map concepts and share their visionary thoughts. Visual aids are their tools of choice to create and share their ideas.

THE CARTOGRAPHER - WHAT YOUR SYMBOL MEANS

The Cartographer symbol comprises three elements: a compass, an angled ruler, and a globe. These are some traditional tools of cartographers. The Cartographer's mark is more specific and focuses on ideas and concepts transformed visually.

The complexity of The Cartographer's symbol is centered around the unity of how they think, represented by a compass. They follow their true north with unchangeable personal values and are true to themselves and others.

The Cartographer also has pragmatic rationality, represented by an angled ruler symbol. Their multifaceted talent finds patterns, different angles and can quickly determine the scope of problems.

The third element is the globe, representing The Cartographer's ability to present solutions from an aerial view. The Cartographer is an expert who can precisely map issues from various corners of their world and transform them into visionary ideas. They combine mapping with new designs to become masterpieces and spread them to multiple parts of their world with one goal of advancing the world of civilization.

HOW CARTOGRAPHERS RECEIVE NEW INFORMATION

The world is your canvas. If a picture tells a thousand words, you'll take the picture every time. Your brain fuel is a color-coded menu of symbols and maps. You see patterns and talk in pictures.

WORDS TO DESCRIBE THE CARTOGRAPHER

- Applying new ideas

- Know what to do, they work out how they can apply it

- Practice according to visuals

- Follow maps to put into action

FAMOUS CARTOGRAPHERS

- Prince Charles

- Steve Jobs

HOW TO UNLOCK YOUR INNER GENIUS - CARTOGRAPHER

WAYS YOU HOOK INTO NEW INFORMATION - YOUR SWEET SPOT

You love a list! Words or pictures, pen on paper or tapping the keyboard, you like to like to jot it down.

KEY LEARNING ATTRIBUTES

- Want to practice and do something

- Actively use the concept

HOW CAN YOU TAP INTO YOUR CARTOGRAPHER GENIUS ZONE

With your aesthetic fitness, you inhale the puzzle pieces before drawing the fitting conclusion.

HARNESS YOUR SPECIFIC LEARNING PREFERENCE

- Sequential Learners

- Logical & Stepwise

- Prefer presentation in a linear and orderly manner

- Instructions in steps

- Learn in linear steps

- Each step follows logically from the last one

- Follow a logical stepwise approach to finding solutions

- Know the specific aspects of the subject but may have difficulty relating them to different subjects

- If a presenter jumps around and skips steps, you may have trouble following.

WAYS TO TURBO-LEARN IN YOUR INNER GENIUS ZONE

No matter how the information is coming to you, power your learning to turbo by:

- Read given material

- Hands-on activities

- Test theories

- Worksheets

- Fact games

- Puzzles

- Drill

THE COMPOSER

YOUR INNER GENIUS ARCHETYPE

		PROCESSING POWER			
		CONNECT	DETAIL	CONSTRUCT	INVENT
BRAIN FUEL PROFILE	VISUAL	THE DECRYPTER	THE SCRIBE	THE CARTOGRAPHER	THE FUTURIST
	AUDITORY	THE NARRATOR	THE VALEDICTORIAN	THE COMPOSER	THE ENERGIZER
	KINESTHETIC	THE CATALYST	THE HOROLOGIST	THE MASON	THE EXPLORER

HOW THE WORLD SEES THE COMPOSER

Composers' honed social abilities empower them to coordinate all parts of the orchestra and inspire the musical story to dance off the page.

THE COMPOSER - WHAT YOUR SYMBOL MEANS

The symbol for The Composer begins at the center with a segno notation icon (the middle S) combined with the unifying symbol that surrounds the segno.

Segno is the sign that marks the beginning or end of a musical repeat. The Composer forms work patterns that coordinate a 'musical' from the beginning to the end of a performance. Their ability to articulate practicalities is limitless. But, if you look more closely, the segno symbol also forms a person who is dancing. The Composer is adept at their life's dance as they move to create solutions. They are firm but gentle as they lead and follow, watching for others around them.

The unifying symbol is an icon that forms a pattern of mutual attachment to each individual socially that forms a unity. Opposing minds are synchronized by The Composer and unified by integrating boundless possibilities.

Combining the segno and the unifying symbol represents The Composer, a virtuoso whose social skills are honed, which empowers them to coordinate all orchestra parts and inspire musical stories to dance from the page.

HOW COMPOSERS RECEIVE NEW INFORMATION

Your life has a soundtrack. You connect to your world through sound and rhythm, the spoken word, and listening to and collaborating with experts. Your brain fuel takes things off the page and communicates them via the airwaves.

WORDS TO DESCRIBE THE COMPOSER

- Tinkering

- Common sense

- Experimenting

- Skills

FAMOUS COMPOSERS

- Jack Welsh

- Maya Angelou

HOW TO UNLOCK YOUR INNER GENIUS - COMPOSER

WAYS YOU HOOK INTO NEW INFORMATION - YOUR SWEET SPOT

What's the story? You actively listen, discuss and engage in the stories of world around you.

KEY LEARNING ATTRIBUTES

- Want to practice and do something

- Actively use the concept

HOW CAN YOU TAP INTO YOUR COMPOSER GENIUS ZONE

Talk to others before you do something new or when you hit a roadblock.

HARNESS YOUR SPECIFIC LEARNING PREFERENCE

- Sequential Learners

- Logical & Stepwise

- Prefer presentation in a linear and orderly manner

- Instructions in steps

- Learn in linear steps

- Each step follows logically from the last one

- Follow stepwise analytical approach to finding solutions

- Know the specific aspects of the subject but may have difficulty relating them to different subjects

- If a presenter jumps around and skips steps, you may have trouble following.

WAYS TO TURBO-LEARN IN YOUR INNER GENIUS ZONE

No matter how the information is coming to you, power your learning to turbo by:

- Read given material

- Hands-on activities

- Test theories

- Worksheets

- Fact games

- Puzzles

- Drill

THE MASON

YOUR INNER GENIUS ARCHETYPE

PROCESSING POWER				
BRAIN FUEL PROFILE		CONNECT	DETAIL	CONSTRUCT	INVENT
	VISUAL	THE DECRYPTER	THE SCRIBE	THE CARTOGRAPHER	THE FUTURIST
	AUDITORY	THE NARRATOR	THE VALEDICTORIAN	THE COMPOSER	THE ENERGIZER
	KINESTHETIC	THE CATALYST	THE HOROLOGIST	THE MASON	THE EXPLORER

HOW THE WORLD SEES THE MASON

A maker at heart, Masons. Outcomes-based, Masons execute the plan and will be sure that they'll get the job done.

THE MASON - WHAT YOUR SYMBOL MEANS

The symbol of The Mason combines the engineer's spring divider icon and the heart. The engineer's spring divider is the icon of a maker with high accuracy and precision. The Mason marks out their projects and can adjust their pathway to completion. Their ability to finely adjust their plan, rotate, and arc to their solution is exemplary.

The Mason helps others to plot their direction. Their hands-on guidance and coaching walk alongside others as they navigate life's valleys and hills.

The heart is an icon representing the energy and enthusiasm The Mason brings to their work, dreams, and passions. They are often the heart of projects because of their practical abilities. The Mason believes so much in their work that they create unique ideas, designs, and results.

The Mason is a designer and planner who puts their heart into their task because they believe in what they are doing and can complete precision projects confidently with a level of perfection admired by those around them.

HOW MASONS RECEIVE NEW INFORMATION

Hands up? Hands down? Just make sure it's hands-on! Get in, get started, get on with it. Your brain fuel is a moving feast of tactile activity.

WORDS TO DESCRIBE THE MASON

- Building

- Thinking and doing

- Creating usability

- Executes or carries out the steps

FAMOUS MASONS

- Christiano Ronaldo

- Rihanna

HOW TO UNLOCK YOUR INNER GENIUS - MASON

WAYS YOU HOOK INTO NEW INFORMATION - YOUR SWEET SPOT

You embody concepts and bring them to life in the way you communicate.

KEY LEARNING ATTRIBUTES

- Want to practice and do something

- Actively use the concept

HOW CAN YOU TAP INTO YOUR MASON GENIUS ZONE

Play is not reserved for children. Play with ideas, play with information, play with how you do things.

HARNESS YOUR SPECIFIC LEARNING PREFERENCE

- Sequential Learners

- Logical & Stepwise

- Prefer presentation in a linear and orderly manner

- Instructions in steps

- Learn in linear steps

- Each step follows logically from the last one

- Follow logical stepwise approach to finding solutions

- Know the specific aspects of the subject but may have difficulty relating them to different subjects

- If a presenter jumps around and skips steps, you may have trouble following.

WAYS TO TURBO-LEARN IN YOUR INNER GENIUS ZONE

No matter how the information is coming to you, power your learning to turbo by:

- Read given material

- Hands-on activities

- Test theories

- Worksheets

- Fact games

- Puzzles

- Drill

THE FUTURIST

YOUR INNER GENIUS ARCHETYPE

		PROCESSING POWER			
		CONNECT	DETAIL	CONSTRUCT	INVENT
BRAIN FUEL PROFILE	VISUAL	THE DECRYPTER	THE SCRIBE	THE CARTOGRAPHER	THE FUTURIST
	AUDITORY	THE NARRATOR	THE VALEDICTORIAN	THE COMPOSER	THE ENERGIZER
	KINESTHETIC	THE CATALYST	THE HOROLOGIST	THE MASON	THE EXPLORER

HOW THE WORLD SEES THE FUTURIST

Futurists have the vision. The prequel to the main event, they can see what's coming and love to run ahead of the pack the show others the way.

233

THE FUTURIST - WHAT YOUR SYMBOL MEANS

The Futurist symbol is formed around the yin-yang symbol combined with a polygonal chain.

The yin yang symbolizes the balance of two opposites with a portion of the opposite element in each section. Since ancient times, the yin-yang is a source of knowledge for all who studied spiritual and scientific methods and is used for all kinds of competing and complementary forces, with the curved line denoting no absolute separation between the two opposites.

The Futurist is represented by the lower yin-yang symbol as the past, represented by the yin-yang round symbol. Its opposite is the future represented by the polygonal yin-yang symbol. With a focus on the future and be one step ahead, The Futurist is an expert at looking at past phenomena and connecting events and options to see what is possible.

The polygonal chain, being multi-angular, represents the many complex interactions and decisions that The Futurist explores when devising the pros and cons of any project, venture, task, or relationship.

The Futurist is a visionary, full of past phenomena knowledge while knowing what to do in the future, and is always one step ahead of others.

HOW FUTURISTS RECEIVE NEW INFORMATION

The world is your canvas. If a picture tells a thousand words, you'll take the picture every time. Your brain fuel is a color-coded menu of symbols and maps. You see patterns and talk in pictures.

WORDS TO DESCRIBE THE FUTURIST

- Adaptation

- Visual Ideation

- Visioning

- Dynamic

FAMOUS FUTURISTS

- Catherine Mattiske

- Pablo Picasso

- Coco Chanel

HOW TO UNLOCK YOUR INNER GENIUS - FUTURIST

WAYS YOU HOOK INTO NEW INFORMATION - YOUR SWEET SPOT

The fastest route to your next big idea is to sketch it down. Envelope, serviette, ticket. Get it out of your head and onto a page.

KEY LEARNING ATTRIBUTES

- Want to try out variations

- Trying them out in life elsewhere

- Identifying reasons to learn more

HOW CAN YOU TAP INTO YOUR FUTURIST GENIUS ZONE

*Zoom out to see the whole picture
before zooming in for context.*

HARNESS YOUR GLOBAL LEARNING PREFERENCE

- Prefer learning by observing the bigger picture

- Are holistic

- Learn in large chunks

- Absorb materials almost randomly without seeing connections, then suddenly 'get it'

- Solve complex problems quickly

- Once they've grasped the big picture can put things together in novel ways but may not explain how they did it

- Have strong sequential abilities AFTER they've grasped the big picture

WAYS TO TURBO-LEARN IN YOUR INNER GENIUS ZONE

No matter how the information is coming to you, power your learning to turbo by:

- Tips, Tricks, Traps

- Personal Action Plan

- Group Action Plan

- Write story or journal

- Brainstorm uses in real life

- Likely challenges in real life

- Opportunities to change/modify process

THE ENERGIZER

YOUR INNER GENIUS ARCHETYPE

		PROCESSING POWER			
		CONNECT	DETAIL	CONSTRUCT	INVENT
BRAIN FUEL PROFILE	VISUAL	THE DECRYPTER	THE SCRIBE	THE CARTOGRAPHER	THE FUTURIST
	AUDITORY	THE NARRATOR	THE VALEDICTORIAN	THE COMPOSER	THE ENERGIZER
	KINESTHETIC	THE CATALYST	THE HOROLOGIST	THE MASON	THE EXPLORER

HOW THE WORLD SEES THE ENERGIZER

Explorers love a chat. These movers and shakers are the sparkplugs of any conversation. Through their combined passion and desire for communications, they influence and drive change.

THE ENERGIZER - WHAT YOUR SYMBOL MEANS

The Energizer combines a power plug and a lip, and it was fashioned into a single flower plant that blooms.

The plug icon defines as a channel of energy that is beneficial for every individual and group surrounding The Energizer. They energize others with their ideas and upbeat personality. They give power to their friends, family, teammates, and work colleagues.

The lip icon symbolizes that The Energizer has a strong desire to communicate. They combine the willingness to share and channel energy through clear communication to become an inspiration for unity.

Their ideas, inventiveness, and ability to harness innovation are represented by the flower symbol's growth. They drive change and strengthen everyone around them through possibility and positivity.

The Energizers always bloom and channel energy to become a movement of change for the people around them.

HOW ENERGIZERS RECEIVE NEW INFORMATION

Your life has a soundtrack. You connect to your world through sound and rhythm, the spoken word, and listening to and collaborating with experts. Your brain fuel takes things off the page and communicates them via the airwaves.

WORDS TO DESCRIBE THE ENERGIZER

- Ideation by discussion

- Seek hidden possibilities

- Critical consideration

- Tips, Tricks, Traps

FAMOUS ENERGIZERS

- Oprah Winfrey

- Jacinda Adern

HOW TO UNLOCK YOUR INNER GENIUS - ENERGIZER

WAYS YOU HOOK INTO NEW INFORMATION - YOUR SWEET SPOT

You love to talk the talk (with as many people as possible). The more you talk to people, the more information you learn.

KEY LEARNING ATTRIBUTES

- Want to try out variations

- Trying them out in life elsewhere

- Identifying reasons to learn more

HOW CAN YOU TAP INTO YOUR ENERGIZER GENIUS ZONE

*Find a community and connect
with others that have similar
interests to you. Share your ideas
and learn from theirs.*

HARNESS YOUR GLOBAL LEARNING PREFERENCE

- Prefer learning by observing the bigger picture

- Are holistic

- Learn in large chunks

- Absorb materials almost randomly without seeing connections, then suddenly 'get it'

- Solve complex problems quickly

- Once they've grasped the big picture can put things together in novel ways but may not explain how they did it

- Have strong sequential abilities AFTER they've grasped the big picture

WAYS TO TURBO-LEARN IN YOUR INNER GENIUS ZONE

No matter how the information is coming to you, power your learning to turbo by:

- Tips, Tricks, Traps

- Personal Action Plan

- Group Action Plan

- Write story or journal

- Brainstorm uses in real life

- Likely challenges in real life

- Opportunities to change/modify process

THE EXPLORER

YOUR INNER GENIUS ARCHETYPE

		PROCESSING POWER			
		CONNECT	DETAIL	CONSTRUCT	INVENT
BRAIN FUEL PROFILE	VISUAL	THE DECRYPTER	THE SCRIBE	THE CARTOGRAPHER	THE FUTURIST
	AUDITORY	THE NARRATOR	THE VALEDICTORIAN	THE COMPOSER	THE ENERGIZER
	KINESTHETIC	THE CATALYST	THE HOROLOGIST	THE MASON	THE EXPLORER

HOW THE WORLD SEES THE EXPLORER

Discovering new territory is where you will find Explorers. They actively engage the world around them to find new ways of doing things. By taking a new approach, new perspective, or untravelled path, they discover untapped potential and drive forward the status quo.

243

THE EXPLORER - WHAT YOUR SYMBOL MEANS

The Explorer symbol fuses two parts, the magnifying glass and compass icons, into one.

The magnifying glass symbol is a symbol used to represent exploration quests. It is the symbol of intellect and connoisseurship and is evident in art from the 18th century. The Explorer appreciates history and their past world to create possibilities. Today augmented reality uses smartphones and other devices as the modern-day magnifying glass to present a computer expanded view of the world.

The compass symbol is a guide to seeking new paths and new perspectives to achieve the highest potential. The Explorer uses the compass to confirm they are moving in the right direction. However, there will be times when the pathway is unclear. Then, their practicality kicks in, and The Explorer uses the magnifying glass to focus and explore the details of their journey to devise the best steps at that moment.

The Explorer knows and believes that the highest level of potential is a process of patient travel. Using their practical hands-on approach, they understand every problem or new perspective on the journey, so they can discover untapped potential and drive forward the status quo.

HOW EXPLORERS RECEIVE NEW INFORMATION

Hands up? Hands down? Just make sure it's hands-on! Get in, get started, get on with it. Your brain fuel is a moving feast of tactile activity.

WORDS TO DESCRIBE THE EXPLORER

- Doing

- Invention

- Learn by trial and error

- Self-discovery

FAMOUS EXPLORERS

- Bethenny Frankel

- Elon Musk

HOW TO UNLOCK YOUR INNER GENIUS - EXPLORER

WAYS YOU HOOK INTO NEW INFORMATION - YOUR SWEET SPOT

You are not afraid to jump in the deep end. It may lead you to a new pathway or new information.

KEY LEARNING ATTRIBUTES

- Want to try out variations

- Trying them out in life elsewhere

- Identifying reasons to learn more

HOW CAN YOU TAP INTO YOUR EXPLORER GENIUS ZONE

Flip it! Rotate it! Paint it red.
Whatever you are doing, energize
it with a new perspective. Discover
a new filter.

HARNESS YOUR GLOBAL LEARNING PREFERENCE

- Prefer learning by observing the bigger picture

- Are holistic

- Learn in large chunks

- Absorb materials almost randomly without seeing connections, then suddenly 'get it'

- Solve complex problems quickly

- Once they've grasped the big picture can put things together in novel ways but may not explain how they did it

- Have strong sequential abilities AFTER they've grasped the big picture

WAYS TO TURBO-LEARN IN YOUR INNER GENIUS ZONE

No matter how the information is coming to you, power your learning to turbo by:

- Tips, Tricks, Traps

- Personal Action Plan

- Group Action Plan

- Write story or journal

- Brainstorm uses in real life

- Likely challenges in real life

- Opportunities to change/modify process

PART 6.
HOW TO
HOOK IN ALL
ARCHETYPES

By now, you've most likely met your own Inner Genius. You may have read about other Archetypes and compared your Archetype with friends, family, and co-workers. So how can you put your new knowledge into action and become the wizard of communication to build *translation bridges* with every other type of Archetype?

Here's where the marvel begins. You can be solidly in your own Inner Genius Archetype, owing to your learning preference. Regardless of how information is given to you, you'll be translating it into your learning language.

In this section, we'll look at how you can work with all Inner Genius Archetypes to become the whizz of *translation bridges* and ace communication with authority!

Here are our 12 Inner Genius Archetypes. Remember that they are matrixed on Brain Fuel Profile and Processing Power

		PROCESSING POWER			
		CONNECT	DETAIL	CONSTRUCT	INVENT
BRAIN FUEL PROFILE	VISUAL	THE DECRYPTER	THE SCRIBE	THE CARTOGRAPHER	THE FUTURIST
	AUDITORY	THE NARRATOR	THE VALEDICTORIAN	THE COMPOSER	THE ENERGIZER
	KINESTHETIC	THE CATALYST	THE HOROLOGIST	THE MASON	THE EXPLORER

Figure 2 - Inner Genius Archetype Matrix

To make it easier, you don't have to memorize anything. As long as you know the hooks to the three Brain Fuel profiles and the four Processing Powers, you'll be the hotshot every time you interact with another Archetype.

Let's dive into this new phenomenon now!

HOW TO WORK WITH THE DECRYPTER, NARRATOR, OR CATALYST

	CONNECT	
VISUAL	THE DECRYPTER	
AUDITORY	THE NARRATOR	
KINESTHETIC	THE CATALYST	

The one thing that the Decrypter, Narrator, and Catalyst have in common is that they all have the **Connect Processing Power**. So, when you are communicating with them, the Inner Genius strategy uses these communication tips and tactics for the Connect Processing Power.

What makes them **different is their Brain Fuel**. Even though they share the Connect Processing Power, ensure that you are using Predicate Phrases and Keywords for each of the Brain Fuel profiles to super-charge your written and spoken communication. As you become more skilled, you'll start to incorporate their Power-Up, but firstly focus on connecting with the Decrypter, Narrator, and Catalyst.

ASK THIS FIRST

What's your experience with this?

WHEN YOU WANT TO TEACH SOMEONE, INCLUDE:

- Activities to build human interaction

- Activities to build respect

- Activities to build trust

- Conversations about the possible meaning

- Discussion

- Finding the 'big idea.'

- Asking: How do you feel about the learning?

- Linking to personal values

- Personal significance, not meaning for others

- Personal, meaningful connections based on experience

- Putting the topic into context

- Shared storytelling to find out the meaning

- The attention grabber - tell them why

TURBO COMMUNICATION - CUSTOMIZE YOUR MESSAGE

A job aid to help people communicate - use these words to hook in your reader:

additional benefit	advantage	advantageousness
asset	asset	belief
benefit	context	definition
drift	explanation	feeling
focus	gain	goal
heart	idea	implication
impression	intention	justification
meaning	merit	motivation
nuance	perspective	point
position	prior knowledge	purpose
return	reward	reward
sense	significance	slant
spirit	strength	symbolization
understanding	upside	usefulness
value	view	view
viewpoint	way of thinking	whole idea
worth	worthiness	

JUST BEFORE YOU FINISH, DID YOU...?

Checksheet to ensure that the communication hooks into each type

Did I....

- articulate the reason why?

- create an opportunity to buy in?

- recognize previous experience?

- link to personal values?

HOW TO WORK WITH THE SCRIBE, VALEDICTORIAN, OR HOROLOGIST

	DETAIL	
VISUAL	THE SCRIBE	
AUDITORY	THE VALEDICTORIAN	
KINESTHETIC	THE HOROLOGIST	

The Scribe, Valedictorian, and Horologist are the rarest of Inner Genius Archetypes. However, with the Detail Processing Power in common, they are driven by detail. So, when you are communicating with them, the Inner Genius strategy uses these communication tips and tactics for the Detail Processing Power.

254

What makes them **different is their Brain Fuel**. Even though they share the Detail Processing Power, ensure that you are using Predicate Phrases and Keywords for each of the Brain Fuel profiles to super-charge your written and spoken communication.

ASK THIS FIRST

What are the facts?

WHEN YOU WANT TO TEACH SOMEONE, INCLUDE:

- Activities to focus on relating and organizing information

- Details that focus on remembering and reciting

- Facts, data, lists, and step-by-step processes and make sure you get straight to the point

- In-depth information

- Lectures (teaching)

TURBO COMMUNICATION - CUSTOMIZE YOUR MESSAGE

A job aid to help people communicate - use these words to hook in your reader:

actuality	approach	basic
blueprint	bottom line	chapter and verse
concrete information	cornerstone	defend
define	degree	describe
detail	evidence	explain
fact-based	foundation	generalize
Identify	illustrate	increment
label	layout	list
match	method	number of

paraphrase	part	principle
proof	reality	recite
recognize	relate	restate
review	size	standard
statistic	substance	summarize
tell	transaction	truth
what	when	where
who	write	

JUST BEFORE YOU FINISH, DID YOU...?

Checksheet to ensure that the communication hooks into each type

Did I....

- explain the data/steps/process clearly?

- have a stepwise plan for execution?

- equip people with all knowledge and information needed?

- provide reference information to other resources or experts?

HOW TO WORK WITH THE CARTOGRAPHER, COMPOSER, OR MASON

	CONSTRUCT	
VISUAL	THE CARTOGRAPHER	
AUDITORY	THE COMPOSER	
KINESTHETIC	THE MASON	

The Cartographer, Composer, and Mason worlds are bound by their Construct Processing Power, driven by doing. So, when you are communicating with them, the Inner Genius strategy uses these communication tips and tactics for the Construct Processing Power.

What makes them **different is their Brain Fuel**. Even though they share the Construct Processing Power, ensure that you are using Predicate Phrases and Keywords for each of the Brain Fuel profiles to super-charge your written and spoken communication.

ASK THIS FIRST

How does it work?

WHEN YOU WANT TO TEACH SOMEONE, INCLUDE:

- Coaching

- Consistent activity 'let them try'

- Constant inquiry

- Focus on applying information according to a specific situation

- Practice in a perfect world before introducing variation (i.e., what's been taught, without any changes or adaptations)

TURBO COMMUNICATION - CUSTOMIZE YOUR MESSAGE

A job aid to help people communicate - use these words to hook in your reader:

accomplish	achievement	application
apply	assemble	bring to fruition
change	commit	complete
conclude	construct	course of action
create	deliver on	design
develop	discover	dummy run
enactment	execution	exercise
experience	fulfillment	generate
get done	implement	implementation
interpret	make	make happen
make it	manufacture	model
negotiate	organize	perform
pursuit	prepare	process
produce	put together	putting into practice
realize	report	run-through
solve	try-out	use
utilization		

JUST BEFORE YOU FINISH, DID YOU...?

Checksheet to ensure that the communication hooks into each type

Did I....

- provide the opportunity to practice?

- provide tools, templates, job aids to help?

- allocate all resources needed?

- coach along the way?

HOW TO WORK WITH THE FUTURIST, ENERGIZER, OR EXPLORER

	INVENT	
VISUAL	THE FUTURIST	
AUDITORY	THE ENERGIZER	
KINESTHETIC	THE EXPLORER	

The vibrant lives of the Futurist, Energizer, and Explorer are unified by their Invent Processing Power which is driven by doing. So, when you are communicating with them, the

Inner Genius strategy uses these communication tips and tactics for the Invent Processing Power.

What makes them **different is their Brain Fuel**. Even though they share the Invent Processing Power, ensure that you are using Predicate Phrases and Keywords for each of the Brain Fuel profiles to super-charge your written and spoken communication.

ASK THIS FIRST

What are the possibilities?

WHEN YOU WANT TO TEACH SOMEONE, INCLUDE:

- Opportunities to celebrate success

- Activities creating interest and desire

- Critical thinking

- Diverse activities

- Evaluating and making judgments based on information

- Times to focus on parts and their functionality to the whole

- Visioning activities - paint a vision for the future - what will the end result look like?

- Exercises to practice new information or processes but build in variation

- Putting parts together in a new way

- Questions that are not easily solved

- Self-discovery

- Surprises as opportunities to extend learning

TURBO COMMUNICATION - CUSTOMIZE YOUR MESSAGE

A job aid to help people communicate - use these words to hook in your reader:

analyze	appraise	assess
blue-sky thinking	brainstorm	buzz session
categorize	classify	combine
compare	conceptualize	concocting
consideration	contrast	convert
creating	critical thinking	criticize
debate	defend	deliberate
diagram	differentiate	disassemble
dreaming up	evolve	examine
exchange	free-thinking	free-association
group-think	huddle	hypothesize
invent	line of thought	merge
metamorphose	problem solve	reality check
reason	recommend	research
round table	separate	solve
subdivide	think	transform
value	weigh	

JUST BEFORE YOU FINISH, DID YOU...?

Checksheet to ensure that the communication hooks into each type

Did I....

- refine and adapt for real-world situations?

- provide tips, tricks, and shortcuts?

- provide traps that people might encounter?

- provide the opportunity to assess gaps?

CONCLUSION

We can take these materials at our highest cognitive levels and arrange and rearrange them constantly to make bigger and better buildings. That is why, as we mentioned earlier, we suggest trying to commit more and more information to memory. The more you have at your disposal, the more you can build later.

Remember (see, there is that word again!) *everything* we have in our memory banks is a potential building block to make something else. Our aim, and one we hope we can impart upon you, is that there is no limit to what you can build once you start putting together these blocks. So when we advocate storage for life, we mean that it is always beneficial to build a stockpile of as many raw materials as you can to build whatever you want, whenever you want, later.

In practice, this can be challenging. When presented with so much information, it can be difficult to store all of it. It can also be challenging to know *what* is worth holding in the first place. Some pieces of information will be intuitive. If there are things you *want* to remember, then you will work toward that end. The trick is to identify components of information that might not be immediately relevant but have the potential for later cognitive "construction." Use your academic instincts to figure out what is worth keeping and what is not. And of course, if something loses relevancy or becomes obsolete, throw it in the wood chipper! Do not waste finite storage space on rotting wood.

Now, let's take a closer look at exactly how our mind stores these essential building blocks. Understanding *how* we remember will make everything we do a little more manageable.

PART 7.

1

MESSAGE

12

ARCHETYPES

Let's switch gears to writing. Not everyone is Ernest Hemingway, Jane Austen, William Shakespeare, or J. K. Rowling. Writing daily text messages, emails, forums, and chat is in direct contrast to academic and formal business writing. It's easy to say that formal writing is dead, but is it? Writing is a skill that is paramount for good communication. Good writing skills give the reader clarity and the ability to communicate to a large audience.

In this section, we'll explore ways to transform your written message, be it an email, report, letter, press release, resume, blog, strategy, or any other written document.

The questions that we'll delve into include:

- What are some quick ways to hook all 12 Inner Genius Archetypes into my written text?

- How can I structure communication for all 12 Inner Genius Archetypes in a logical flow?

- How can I build a training program or workshop topic that creates balance for different learning preferences?

- Are there secrets to starting and finishing presentations and workshops that will 'wow' my audience?

- How can I unlock social learning?

YOUR GOAL: BALANCED COMMUNICATION ACROSS THE INNER GENIUS ARCHETYPE MATRIX

BRAIN FUEL PROFILE	PROCESSING POWER			
	CONNECT	**DETAIL**	**CONSTRUCT**	**INVENT**
VISUAL	THE DECRYPTER	THE SCRIBE	THE CARTOGRAPHER	THE FUTURIST
AUDITORY	THE NARRATOR	THE VALEDICTORIAN	THE COMPOSER	THE ENERGIZER
KINESTHETIC	THE CATALYST	THE HOROLOGIST	THE MASON	THE EXPLORER

Figure 3 - Inner Genius Archetype Matrix

As you work through this section, keep in mind the Inner Genius Archetype Matrix. You've already unlocked your Inner Genius Archetype. The challenge that is before you now is to write in a way that builds translation bridges between you and every other Archetype in a single message.

Once you get the hang of it, you'll be astounded at how easy it is. Yes, it takes practice, but you'll get there. Once you arrive at your new level of competence, you'll start every email, report, presentation, and letter differently.

Get ready now. A new world awaits. Let's go!

QUICK TIPS TO HOOK READERS INTO WHAT YOU WRITE

Even the most gifted intellectual minds sometimes have trouble writing. When you think about it, this makes sense because writing is a skill that leans heavily on particular types of brain processes that not everyone happens to naturally have. Being "smart" does not mean that you can simply overcome the biological realities that we now know dictate so much of our mental capacity.

Luckily, the good news is that being aware of these biological realities means that we can better overcome those that hamper us and capitalize on the ones that naturally work in our favor. We also can find shortcuts when needed. Even those not naturally inclined to generate writing to hook readers, this chapter will provide some helpful tips that anyone can use.

This section will go over some of the ways strong writers captivate their audiences and see if we can mimic some of those actions when composing written works. Yes, spelling and grammar are essential, and all the I's must be dotted and T's crossed. Still, there are other important considerations to think about when putting pen to paper. Let's discuss some of those now, as they will go a long way in helping you deliver on-point messaging every time.

7 WRITING TIPS FOR SPELLBINDING EMAILS, PROPOSALS & REPORTS

TIP #1: SPEAK TO YOUR AUDIENCE

It is effortless to forget who you are writing to when you are writing. Unfortunately, many writers want to cram chunks of big, fancy words to impress their readers and sound-wise. This can be problematic for a few reasons.

First, many times this backfires, and the message becomes foggy and convoluted. Ultimately, the writer actually looks foolish in these instances.

Second, even when the prose is technically composed correctly, the audience may not need (or want) to be bombarded with a virtual thesaurus. Strong messaging gives the audience a clear, direct transmission of an idea without getting a headache along the way. You'll need to clearly articulate the benefit, advantages and connect with the audience for them to really pay attention.

This tip hooks in The Decrypter, Narrator, and Catalyst

THE DECRYPTER	
THE NARRATOR	
THE CATALYST	

TIP #2: TELL STORIES

Stories, as we discussed earlier in the book, are compelling. They are one of the oldest forms of communication in existence. They have endured thousands of years for a good reason; people like them.

Stories are relatable. Stories are digestible. When you hear a story, you are naturally inclined to follow along and put yourself in the character's shoes. When you are writing, use this to your advantage. Use stories to illustrate your points and use them to put your information in context. Not only will this help you deliver your message more effectively, but it will also serve to entertain your audience as well. This is an integral part of effective writing and communication.

This tip hooks in The Decrypter, Narrator, and Catalyst

THE DECRYPTER	
THE NARRATOR	
THE CATALYST	

TIP #3: BE AN EXPERT

People look to referential sources for good, helpful information that will help them accomplish something. When a person picks up a text, there is an understanding that it will be factually correct, accurate, and informative. Give them that!

To truly deliver a solid message to your reader, you must be an expert in that message. You will never show anyone how to do anything if you do not know how to do it well yourself. Expertise is king when it comes to good writing. Know what you are talking about and deliver something valuable and poignant for your reader.

This tip hooks in The Scribe, Valedictorian, and Horologist

THE SCRIBE	
THE VALEDICTORIAN	
THE HOROLOGIST	

TIP #4: DON'T DAWDLE

This is perhaps the most crucial idea any writer needs to think about when crafting a message. So many writers, especially young ones, think that more words mean more successful writing. This could not be farther from the truth. Padding your word count might be helpful when writing a middle school essay, but in real life, no one has the time (nor mental energy) to read a bunch of words they do not need. So get to the point, say what you mean to say, and move on. Less is more when it comes to writing.

This tip will hook in The Scribe, Valedictorian, and Horologist

THE SCRIBE	
THE VALEDICTORIAN	
THE HOROLOGIST	

TIP #5: BACK IT UP

One particularly good way to grab and keep your readers' attention is to provide them concrete examples and evidence of whatever it is you are trying to impart onto them. People want to see how the information they are being given can be applied in practice. They also want to see information first-hand and sourced. Back up your argument, and you will be much further along in making your case than if you left the reader wondering what the basis for your view might be.

This tip hooks in The Scribe, Valedictorian, and Horologist

THE SCRIBE	
THE VALEDICTORIAN	
THE HOROLOGIST	

TIP #6: BE RELEVANT

This one sounds like it is a no-brainer, but many people miss the mark when it comes to relevancy. This can be for a few reasons, but the most common, perhaps, if that the information they are offering is outdated. Information moves at the speed of light—literally; you must also move at the speed of light (good thing we are overcharging our brains!)

Doing this effectively ties into some of the other tips we discussed above. Intense research that is up to date and contextualized will go a long, long way in helping to grab and hold your reader's attention. Suppose you want to compete in the jungle of information exchange. In that case, you must give your readers something they will not be able to get anywhere else.

This tip hooks in The Cartographer, Composer, and Mason

THE CARTOGRAPHER	
THE COMPOSER	
THE MASON	

TIP #7: PROVIDE DEVIATIONS

Ensure that you add real-life situations where rigidity can be changed or challenged when you are writing about a system, process, procedure, or information step-wise.

Acknowledging that 'real life' often happens and that rigorous methods need to be counteracted or disregarded to accommodate the real world is essential to give strength to your message.

Doing this effectively will help verify your deep thinking into what you are communicating. Miss this step at your peril because all the while your audience is hearing or reading your wisdom, they are also applying it to their practical world and materializing it for themselves.

This tip hooks in The Futurist, Energizer, and Explorer

THE FUTURIST	
THE ENERGIZER	
THE EXPLORER	

IN SUMMARY

With these tips, you will create compelling prose that does not hinge on being a naturally gifted writer. All you have to do is give the reader with they want, efficiently and effectively, and do your best not to waste their time. This is achievable! You are, without a doubt, going to be able to do exactly that in no time flat!

STRUCTURING COMMUNICATION FOR 12 ARCHETYPES

In the last chapter, we gave you a guide for some super quick tips to add your secret sauce to your communication on the fly.

In this chapter, we will take you behind the curtain of the most effective communicators who are the alchemists of building *translation bridges* between their personal *Inner Genius Archetype* and everyone else!

We'll introduce you to The *Inner Genius Wheel*. When you read this, we hope that you'll print it, laminate it, frame it, and use it every day as you craft your next presentation, training program, report, sales proposal, or email.

Regardless of whether you are presenting in front of thousands at a convention or symposium, talking to your colleagues in a small meeting, teaching a class, talking to your children, writing a multi-million dollar sales proposal, or an email, The *Inner Genius Wheel* is your blueprint for communication.

Inner Genius is totally unlocked!

THE INNER GENIUS WHEEL

You might be thinking, 'how do I put this all together?"
We're glad you asked.

Let's say you have a report, a training workshop, a presentation, or some other form of communication. You want to dazzle your audience with your ability to hook in every type of Inner Genius Archetype so that they'll be hanging on your every written or spoken word.

What about if you are a parent? There is a way to speak to all of your children at the same time to gain their attention with equality of understanding.

Are you a sports coach? One message that will work for every player? That would be amazing.

Impossible, we hear you say!

Hang onto your hats! Take the 'im' out of impossible, and you'll get 'possible.' Not only is it possible, but it's also straightforward. You'll be able to do it today. Yes – in your next email, letter, report, presentation, training workshop, or wherever you are communicating, you can use it.

Introducing the *Inner Genius Wheel*. It's your Inner Genius blueprint for communication. Like a clock, you start at 12 o'clock. You'll write or say your message following **in order** Connect, Detail, Construct, then Invent, and in so doing, hook every one of the 12 Inner Genius Archetypes into your message.

SHORT COMMUNICATION – EMAILS, LETTERS, AND SALES PROPOSALS

USING THE *INNER GENIUS WHEEL* TO STRUCTURE GENERAL COMMUNICATION

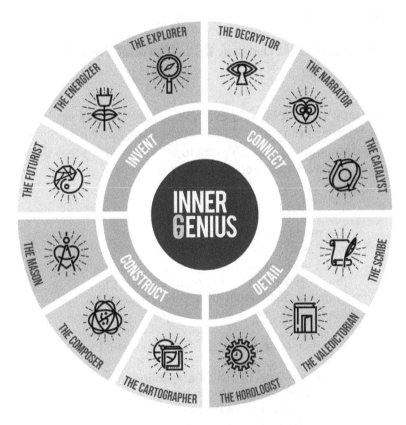

You're in a rush. You open a new email, slam out your thoughts, quickly re-read it to ensure that you've covered all of your points, spell check, and press 'send.'

The email made complete sense to you, and then a flurry of questions come back to you, along with some gripes and negativity. What went wrong? Chances are you communicated in your Inner Genius Archetype language.

But, as you can see from the *Inner Genius Wheel*, that's only 1/12th of the opportunity.

Don't beat yourself up. You've probably been doing it all your life, and now with your newly unlocked Inner Genius, you might be reflecting back on all of those missed opportunities.

Let's fix this now.

COMPARING NATURAL LANGUAGE WITH *INNER GENIUS WHEEL* COMMUNICATION

Let's look at the following example. A short email stating a new business direction. Conor is a leader, and he wants to send one email to all 1,250 employees to clearly state the newly acquired business. It's super exciting.

> Hi team
>
> You might have heard the news that ABC purchased XYZ company last week. After much negotiation, we successfully purchased the US and European operations for $10m. That included their manufacturing facility and operational team.
>
> This type of deal is unheard of in our industry.
>
> Congratulations to Mark, Cara, Charlotte, Jahi, Kobe, and Keisha for the many hours they worked to harmonize the offer. We can't sing their praises enough!
>
> If you want to take a look at the deal, you'll find it in the "Acquisitions" files. Then, if you have any questions, tune into my next leadership presentation.
>
> Great news!
> Conor

Can you spot Conor's Inner Genius Archetype?

Notice the detailed language and the brain fuel predicate phrases.

Conor is the Valedictorian. His propensity for detail coupled with Auditory Brain Fuel language is a giveaway. So he's talking beautifully to the other Valedictorians in his organization. But what about the different 11 Archetypes?

Let's restructure Conor's email using the *Inner Genius Wheel.*

Hi team

We've achieved the last step of our business goal for this year. In our Vision Report, you'll recall that we set out to acquire an organization that could give us expanded manufacturing and operational facilities. We've all been stretched in this area, so I'm thrilled to announce our latest acquisition.

CONNECT

Last week ABC purchased XYZ company for $10m effective within 90 days. The acquisition includes the US and European operations, including their manufacturing facility and operational team. (If you want to take a look at the deal, you'll find it in the "Acquisitions" files.)

DETAIL

The deal spanned 120 days headed by Mark and assisted by Cara, Charlotte, Jahi, Kobe, and Keisha. Their tireless work to build a win: win deal that grows our current business was outstanding. We can't sing their praises enough! Congratulations!

CONSTRUCT

All of us will be involved in the integration of XYZ, its people, and its processes. We're going to need to be creative as we map new ways of working. I'll need all of your creativity and innovation to be switched to 'high' during the transition.

INVENT

If you have any questions, come along to my next leadership presentation, join us on the Leadership Live two-way chat, or jot a note on the team board.

It's an exciting day for the growth of ABC!

See you soon!
Conor

Conor has not let go of his Valedictorian Inner Genius. However, this communication cycles through the Inner Genius Wheel in order.

It also uses a balance of Brain Fuel predicate phrases, ensuring that everyone is hooked in.

Regardless of each individual employee's Inner Genius Archetype, Connor is speaking to them in their way. He's built *translation bridges* by using all of the Brain Fuel Profiles and the Processing Power. Using the *Inner Genius Wheel,* the message is inspiring, detailed, unifying, and supportive.

BUILDING TOPICS FOR FORMAL LEARNING & PRESENTATIONS

Congratulations! You have conquered quick communication, like emails, letters, and reports. Now, let's explore longer communications such as training workshops, presentations, and more comprehensive reports.

In this chapter, we will guide you through creating topics of learning using the *Inner Genius Wheel.* You can use a similar process for presentations and written reports. Your design thinking has been done, and it's now time for the construction steps to begin.

This book is not intended as a complete guide on how to design learning. But, here is a sneak peek of the ID9 Workshop Flow that trainers, teachers, facilitators, and subject matter experts learn as their entry into the world of ID9 Intelligent Design.

If you'd like to know more about our Workshop Creation Masterclass, click here for more information and registration details:

https://www.id9intelligentdesign.com/id9-masterclasses/

Your 'learning construction.'

The ID9 Intelligent Design "Build Workflow" develops the program in full, according to your Blueprint and Brochure.

ID9 MASTERCLASS BUILD WORKFLOW

MODEL
ROADMAP
BUILD
ENGAGE
FINISH
BOOST
THE JOURNEY
PARTICIPANT PACK
CHECKLIST
TIE A BOW
SHOWTIME
CELEBRATE

For this book, let's focus on just one of those steps: Build. This step is used to Build Topics. We'll give you a super-fast short version so that you can get started today. And when you are ready for more, consider enrolling in the ID9 Workshop Creation Masterclass or one of the Certified ID9 Professional programs. You'll find all of the information here:

The second step of the ID9 Intelligent Design Build is **'Build.'**

The goal of Build is to **create all learning topics, perfectly balanced according to adult learning preferences.**

https://www.id9intelligentdesign.com/

USING THE *INNER GENIUS WHEEL* TO BUILD TOPICS

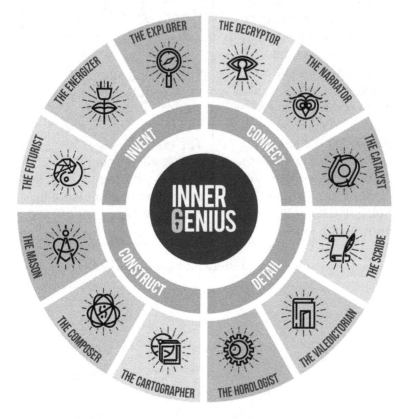

Instead of opening PowerPoint or Google Slides and cramming in your content, **stop** and think. You have the opportunity to hook in every Inner Genius Archetype in every topic that you present, train, or facilitate.

It sounds elementary to say, 'build each topic one at a time.' However, this is a major downfall for many people. They dabble in creating many topics at once and fall into one of two significant traps.

TRAP 1 - THE VORTEX OF CONTENT

People's first trap is getting sucked into the Vortex of Content, meaning they get overwhelmed with the amount of content they have and keep adding content incessantly. The result usually looks like 100 PowerPoint slides, they can't see the wood for the trees, and they get completely overwhelmed.

I call that being sucked into the vortex of content or being **Lost Down a Rabbit Hole**; you can't get out because there's just so much content to deal with.

So we want to avoid that trap at all costs.

TRAP 2 - THE GLITZY BRIGHT LIGHTS OF GRAPHIC DESIGN

The other trap that we want to avoid is the **Glitzy Bright Lights of Graphic Design**.

It is natural to want to create a participant-facing finished product. It makes us feel productive and provides a sense of accomplishment. At this point, during the initial Build, it's too early to do this.

What generally happens is that people want to create their finished PowerPoint slides or handouts, so they go online, look for great photos, start their slides or documents, and the design takes them forever. While creating these assets may feel good for a while, what happens is people lose the big picture of the topics they are building. When they come back to reality and finish building their topics, most likely, their graphic design needs altering or discarding all together because their content has changed.

While it may be tempting to start creating participant-facing documents or slides, hold back, and you'll save time and effort and stay on the productive ID9 Intelligent Design fast-track.

ACTIVITY 1 - DESIGN CONTENT FOR EACH TOPIC

*Remember! You will use one
rotation of the Inner Genius Wheel
for <u>every topic</u>.*

TIP FOR SUCCESS:

Begin with your first topic and focus entirely on that topic.
Then, finish each topic in turn before moving to the next.
This will ensure that you maintain focus and will be the
most productive and efficient method of building topics.
Taking on each and every topic simultaneously can be
overwhelming, which is why the smaller breakdown of each
topic is essential. It makes the overall task achievable
without seeming burdensome.

In **Activity 1 – Design Content for Each Topic,** you'll build
the content (what we train) and process (how we teach it)
for every topic. This will help in giving direction and
concreteness to the goals you have envisioned. When
content is decided and allocated for each topic, you will
know what is being covered and the achievable goals
alongside.

Follow these steps IN ORDER. It's essential for maximized
learning that you tackle each topic (each chunk of content)
in the order of the *Inner Genius Wheel*

4-STEP PROCESS TO DESIGN BALANCED INNER GENIUS TOPICS

INNER GENIUS WHEEL STEP	INNER GENIUS ARCHETYPE FOCUS	DEFINITION	TIPS FOR SUCCESS
1 – Write the 'Connect	The Decrypter The Narrator The Catalyst	For your training program or presentation Create a reason for learning. Why is it necessary for participants to know this information? How will it help them? What do they know of this already?	Put yourself in the participant's shoes. What is the benefit/ advantage of them learning this topic? Think in their terms: what's the big win for them if they know this?
2 – Write the 'Detail'	The Scribe The Valedictorian The Horologist	For your training program or presentation, create the steps and sequence… What are the steps involved? What is the relationship from one part to another? What are the priorities? What is the order?	What are the must-knows of this topic that participants MUST learn to reach their mini-goal? Tip: Try to focus on the 'must-knows', rather than the 'should-knows', or 'nice to knows.'

3 – Write the 'Construct	The Cartographer The Composer The Mason	For your training program or presentation create the practice and personalization ... How can the participants be involved in the learning? How does this work? How can they try it? What worksheets could I create?	Look back at your 'What'. What is it that Participants need to practice? Refer to your mini-goal. What do they need to DO in the workshop to achieve your mini-goal?
4 – Write the 'Invent'	The Futurist The Energizer The Explorer	For your training program create the change or challenge... What can they discover themselves? What can their learning become? What are the tips, tricks, and traps? How can they add something themselves?	Look back at your 'What.' What else do Participants need to know. Perhaps add in some 'should-knows', or 'nice to knows' as tips, tricks, and traps. Or create an opportunity for them to add their own real-life situations into the topic. Keep this simple. Chances are they've already achieved your mini-goal during the 'What' section, so this is simply icing on the cake!

ACTIVITY 2 - LEARNING BALANCE & MATERIALS

In **Activity 2 – Learning Balance & Materials,** the ID9 Content Mapping Tool will be used to check the 'hooks' for different Brain Fuel profiles – Visual, Auditory, and Kinesthetic, and create a list of the physical or digital materials required for each topic.

Being inclusive in your approach to teaching is very important. You want to create something that would be conducive to learning for everyone. Incorporating individual differences in Brain Fuel will help in the long run. It is different from standardized education, where one size fits all approach is used. We're trying to make things work, do something better here. So make sure to include all other Brain Fuel profiles and materials within this to better cater to everyone.

While you're at it, try gathering more materials for different Brain Fuel profiles. For that, you will need to unleash your creativity and brainstorm ideas on how all other modalities can be incorporated. Refer to the Brain Fuel section of this guide to help you spark ideas.

CHECKPOINT	HOW TO DO THIS
Now check the balance of Brain Fuel profiles for your training topic.	Source this from Activity 1 – Build Content for Each Topic. From a participant's perspective during the Connect, Detail, Construct and Invent, note What do they hear? What do they see? And what do they do during this topic?
	For Auditory - What did they hear from me, the trainer, and hear from other participants in the group. List activities.

	For Visual - What did they see the trainer present (e.g., slides, flipcharts, etc.), and see within the workshop (other participants, handouts, job aids, etc.). List visual elements. For Kinesthetic - What did they physically do (List individual, paired, small group and whole-group activities).
What materials do you need to run this topic? (e.g., handouts, visual aids, wall charts, etc.)	Source this from Activity 1 – Build Content for Each Topic. List the assets that need to be created for this topic. List all materials required. You do not have to create them now. You could choose to build these later.

6 SECRETS FOR POWERFUL TRAINING AND MEETING OPENINGS

STANDARD AND PREDICTABLE? NOT FOR INNER GENIUSES

We've all been to the training program, workshop or meeting that starts off with, "Welcome to part 1 of xyz, I'm Sally, and I am going to be the teacher/facilitator/trainer/host today. Turn off your cellphones, grab a glass of water, and let me know if you need a break to refresh your mind." Sally then proceeds to go through a list of housekeeping items for 10-minutes, including a bit of herself and her background. She ends it with a 'let's get started' and tries to say it with as much enthusiasm as possible because she knows you're already bored.

This is so standard and predictable that even if the information is exciting in nature, you're already bored. You're thinking about your emails, the work you could be doing instead of sitting in on this training, or daydreaming about what you're going to do when the presentation is done.

The thing is, if Sally were to approach you differently, this preprogramming could change with some tricks, tips, and techniques for the first couple of minutes. All training and presentation where adults are in the audience need to be based on adult learning theory and principles, helping you to really immerse yourself in the content so you feel alert and enthusiastic about the content at hand.

START WITH THE FIRST AND LAST PIECE OF INFORMATION

When designing courses, coaching, and mentoring, it's essential to understand the basics of the ID9 Intelligent Design learning design system: primacy and recency. In essence, 'people remember best, what they hear first and last.'

Think about it. Primacy relates to the information that was presented first, while recency relates to the information presented most recently (i.e., the last thing you most recently heard/learned). The recency effect results in a better recall of the most recent information. When paired with primacy, it tends to be the only two things you are probably going to take away from the presentation. Therefore, professional development training needs to take these realities into account.

PRIMACY AND RECENCY

Sousa, David. A 2011 book on 'How the brain learns' described Primacy and Recency Sousa suggests one factor affecting retention is the primacy-recency effect – essentially, the idea that in a "learning episode," we recall the things that came first (primacy) and the things that came last (recency) better than we recall the things in the middle.[11]

---

[11] https://en.wikipedia.org/wiki/Serial-position_effect

Several of Sousa's points can be summarized in an ideal learning design system, outlined below:

1. **Teach the New Material First:** This isn't just stating the obvious. Sousa gives the example of an English teacher asking a class what *onomatopoeia* is. There's a brief discussion with lots of wrong answers (because the students had no idea). But the students wrote those wrong answers on the subsequent test – partly because they occurred in that initial period. This kind of teaching format captures more attention. It acts as an assessment tool to measure learning outcomes that your team can observe for new corporate training programs down the line.

2. **Use the Prime Time Wisely: Prime Time is the minutes that form the start and end of a learning session.** Even with the best of intentions, teachers can do the following: after commanding focus by telling the class the day's lesson objective, the teacher takes attendance, distributes the previous day's homework, collects that days' homework, requests notes from absent students, and reads an announcement about a club meeting after school. As a finale, the teacher tells the students they were so well-behaved during the lesson that they can do anything they want during the last five minutes of class (i.e., during prime time, as long as they are quiet).

   How many training sessions in business have you endured with a similar pattern? They start with, "today we're going to learn how to effectively plan sales campaigns, or let's start here from so-and-so in the sales department," or, "look at these sales figures from 2005." And, they may end with, "Let's have an early mark, please complete your evaluation forms, and then you can go." Unfortunately, in this business example, Prime Time is underutilized with primacy and recency opportunities wasted.

3. **Retention Varies with Length of Episode.** "As the lesson time lengthens, the percentage of down-time [when retention is at its lowest] *increases faster than for the prime -times.*" Shorter (in general) is better. And varying the type of activity, the instructional method, or even the topic between peak periods is beneficial to learning. Learning and development specialists base their entire training design and development around brevity, knowing that the brain works in 'sprints' when gathering and remembering information. Countless studies have detailed what happens with retention when training times drag on.[12]

12

http://www.lancsngfl.ac.uk/secondary/math/download/file/How%20the%20Brain%20Learns%20by%20Davi
d%20Sousa.pdf

6 SECRETS FOR POWERFUL TRAINING AND MEETING OPENINGS

THE LANGUAGE AND STRUCTURE OF THE SENSATIONAL MEETING OPENING

Let's go back to the foundations of learning experience design to capture the audiences' attention. Your welcome should take two minutes or less. If you are unsure of how long it is taking, rehearse it at home with a timer. The more you practice, the more you will learn that even one minute is a lot of time for a welcome.

Your welcome says to listeners who you are and why they should or should not pay attention to what you are saying. Unfortunately, the people who drone on during a meeting opening are losing the opportunity to harness the attention of attendees.

What should be included in this meeting welcome? We're glad you asked!

1. **Let Go of Your Outdated Ideas:** Do you remember the story of Sally? Don't be a Sally. Remember how she talked about herself, mindless housekeeping (which everyone knows), and nothing about the benefits and advantages of what's in her presentation? The innovative future is here, and it's time to embrace it.

   This technique will make you stand out and power your pathway to extraordinary success.

297

2. **Start Traditional and then Dive into the Big Picture:** People love stories. You can state your name and who you are but then dive into a story. Articulate the end goal of the program by tying it into a captivating tale.

This technique will hook in The Decrypter, The Narrator, and The Catalyst

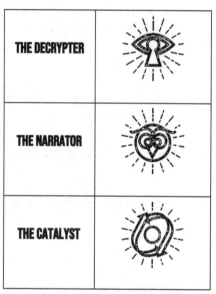

THE DECRYPTER	
THE NARRATOR	
THE CATALYST	

3. **Capture Attention, Then Go Formal:** Start with eye-catching quotes, facts, and figures that get them thinking. For example, you can say, 'over the past two months, we have lost 35% of our market share to our closest competitor. If we don't act soon, we will go under in over one year. This is not an option for you and me, which is why we must come together to craft this new future. You are a key player in this victory, which is why I am ready to show you what we need to do today. Are you with me?'

This technique will hook in The Decrypter, Narrator, and Catalyst

THE DECRYPTER	
THE NARRATOR	
THE CATALYST	

4. **Do Your Prep Work:** You should be preparing for this presentation days in advance so that you are ready to perform when the lights are on. Send out reminders to people who are joining and make the reminders fun with a quiz or two.

This technique will hook in The Scribe, Valedictorian, and Horologist

THE SCRIBE	
THE VALEDICTORIAN	
THE HOROLOGIST	

5. **Start Before You Start:** The show has begun when the first person arrives in the room (whether virtual or actual). Too many presenters and trainers ignore participants as they enter the physical or virtual room. Think about welcoming someone into your home. You'd never just ignore them until the 'official start time' of your dinner or party!

Design an activity for them to engage with. Having something prepared gives people an opportunity to engage and connect with others. And for you, the presenter, don't just ignore them awkwardly in the corner. Ensure that you greet everyone individually (as much as possible) and welcome them personally to the meeting, presentation or course. If you hide away waiting for the start time, THAT will become their first impression, which is not something you want to promote.

This technique will hook in The Cartographer, Composer, and Mason

THE CARTOGRAPHER	
THE COMPOSER	
THE MASON	

6. **Be Completely Unexpected:** Music, lights, singing, dancing, weird GIFs on the screen, home videos... you name it, if it is unexpected, do it.

This technique will hook in The Futurist, Explorer, and Explorer

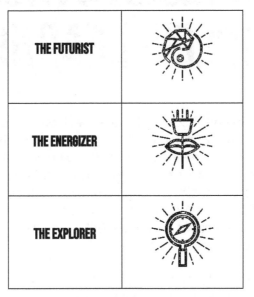

THE FUTURIST	
THE ENERGIZER	
THE EXPLORER	

Bonus tip for virtual learning tools: *for presentations conducted online today, you need to ramp up the energy and shock factor since the distractions are at an all-time high.*

SENDING MESSAGES TO UNLOCK OTHER PEOPLE'S LEARNING

Much of what we discussed in the previous sections deal primarily with how you can obtain and process information. As such, we are working on supercharging your Inner Genius with all sorts of great tips, tricks, and strategies. It is essential to consider, though, that we can reciprocate the benefits of turbo-charged genius with those around us. This is a great benefit for others, but it also has tremendous value for us as well.

Why is that? Well, for one, anytime we engage the mental processes aimed at strengthening our minds, whether it is directed inward or outward, we exercise the muscles in our minds. These mental gymnastics is critical to ensuring we have a well-rounded, robust and active sense. All told, education is a give and take proposition. It is almost impossible to completely isolate one from the other.

So, what are some ways to use our outflow of mental energy to boost others around us? First, it is instrumental in finding learners with commonalities closely aligned to your own personal learning profile and traits. Second, with these partners, we can "send messages" to one another that act as learning conduits.

If you have Visual Brain Fuel, seek out others who retain information in this way and explore movies, artwork, and symbols. For those who have Auditory Brain Fuel and are inclined to listen, take in a concert or speaking engagement with another like learner and enjoy a lengthy conversation to parse through what you heard. Discussion is the ally of the Auditory Brain Fuel. Finally, of course, Kinesthetic Brain Fuel learners would stand to benefit significantly from engaging in board games, puzzles, and model building with a partner.

In these interactions, you will find an excellent opportunity for mutual growth. This is because human beings are naturally social creatures. As a result, we have a strong capacity for recharging each other through socialization, teamwork, and cooperation.

EXERCISES FOR SOCIALIZED LEARNING

There are many ways to connect with learners who are similar to you. Here are some ideas that you can put into play immediately to supercharge your Inner Genius:

- Join a book club or a film club

- Find a friend who is looking to learn a new skill or hobby and become their mentor

- Find online chatrooms/clubs with individuals who share your interests

- Start/Join an environmental group

- Join a sports league

- Take online courses in a new subject area

- Give free lessons for community members in a subject area you have expertise in

PART 8. STORAGE FOR LIFE

Here, we will dive into how all of this information, once transmitted, is actually stored and used. To that end, we will look at the differences between the different types of memories we have available to us.

Let's quickly touch upon the different types of memory before we dive more deeply into how they interact with one another. We have available to us our:

- **Intermediate memory**

- **Working memory**

- **Long-term memory**

These memories are all related to each other, but they are ultimately separated in physical, biological, and functionality. Memory, at all three stages, is an integral part of learning. We rely on the information we have stored to do everything from making a sandwich to building a successful business.

Memory is the foundation for growth. For example, we cannot learn how to make a sandwich, to keep with the above-stated example, if we cannot remember essential information like where the bread and cheese are stored. Similarly, we cannot run a successful business if we cannot remember things like how to do basic math and record-keeping. Simply stated, we must remember the high-level, complex pieces of information that we have learned and the smaller ones that we often take for granted.

This is a building process. We remember how to add so that we can learn how to calculate profit and overhead. Extrapolated out, this concept is essential when we are discussing ways to achieve long-term success. Think about, say, a trip we take to a large professional conference or summit. There will be dozens of presenters, networking opportunities, and pieces of literature to consider. Will we remember all of it? Probably not, but that is OK. What we do retain, though, are going to be valuable pieces of information that we can store for use later.

Now, we might not need each building block right away. Imagine you were literally building things with the blocks of information you received at the summit. You may have learned a new accounting method or advertising tactic at the conference and will put them to work right away constructing your current organization. You are building with that information now.

Also, consider, though, that you might also be collecting some mental lumber for another "building" you want to put together later. Perhaps you found some great piece of emerging tech at this summit that is not directly relevant to your current business operation. You think it is promising, though, so you "store" it away at your lumber yard. Then, when the time comes to construct with it, it will be there, ready and waiting for you to use.

ACCESSING LEARNING SPEED

TALKING SPEED VS. LISTENING SPEED

Talking Speed and listening speed are two areas that many people do not think about when discussing education, pedagogy (children's learning) and andragogy (adult learning). Still, they are equal parts, both exciting and vital.

In short, people listen a lot faster than people talk. Let that sink in for a second because it is not entirely intuitive. To add further possibilities of miscommunication, we listen faster than we speak. When you are talking to someone, it is likely you could be giving them more information faster and would still be able to process that information effectively.

FAST LISTENING VS. SLOW SPEAKING

LISTENING VS. SPEAKING RATE

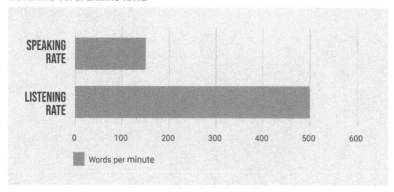

The average person speaks at a rate of 100-200 words per minute. Let's say that's an average of 150 words per minute, for example. The average person listens at a rate of 500 words per minute.

Therefore, when you are listening to someone speak, your brain could process a further 350 words per minute.

Therefore, we have a lot of time thinking about other things – not necessarily what the speaker is saying!

Think about the types of occasions that you have tuned out, either accidentally or on purpose.

THE IMPACT FOR LEARNING

So, what does this mean when it comes to education and information transmission?

It means that if people have the capacity for more information faster, they might crave that information. If we are not going to deliver on the extra information they have the ability to take in, we better at least make what we are saying worth listening to! Relatively slow, uninteresting data does no one any good. Therefore, it is necessary to make what you are saying really motivational and impactful to speed up learning. Otherwise, we risk the people drifting off.

To be clear, we are not advocating you start rushing through every conversation and talk at people a mile a minute. However, this is socially off-putting, even if it is not particularly biologically problematic.

Instead, the better tactic is to simply make what we are saying more meaningful. We will talk more about this later, but it is crucial to eliminate waste in both writing and speaking. Human beings simply are not interested in white noise when it comes to learning. Stick to the relevant information and deliver it crisply.

Further, it is even more critical to deploy pithy messaging as information consumers now have a diminishing attention span and are faced with a seemingly overwhelming (you could easily substitute the word intimidating here as well) amount of data.

Therefore, strong, effective audio communication hinges on efficiency. Keep this in mind as you go about your educational journey.

INTERMEDIATE MEMORY VS. WORKING MEMORY VS LONG-TERM MEMORY

Earlier in this book, we touched upon the biological considerations concerning human memory. A naturally crucial part of learning—knowing something does little good if we cannot retain it—memory is equal parts complex and critical.

THREE TYPES OF MEMORY

One thing that makes the memory so interesting is that it has multiple components that all work quite differently. They are **intermediate memory, working memory,** and **long-term memory**. Learning & Memory, an excellent scientific resource, can help us identify and understand those different components.[13]

"Immediate memory refers to the limited amount of information that can be held in mind when the material is presented for learning. Working memory refers to the capacity to maintain this limited amount of information through active rehearsal, usually across a relatively short

---

[13] http://learnmem.cshlp.org/content/19/1/15.full.html

time interval (Baddeley and Hitch 1974). Long-term memory refers to what can be recalled from the past when the information to be learned no longer occupies the current stream of thought, either because immediate memory capacity was exceeded or because attention was diverted from the memoranda," reads the scientific journal.

NOT EVERYTHING IS STORED EQUALLY

As you can see, we do not store all information equally. To learn something— and by learning, we mean the process by which new data is permanently stored in our mind—each of these parts of our memory must do their part and work together. Learning only comes, in earnest, when information is transmitted across each of these segments of memory before being ultimately stored in our memory banks permanently.

One of the most important things we can do as learners is commit to processing new data so that it ends up being stored permanently for later use. In other words, we must consciously work on moving data from one type of memory to another. If you have ever heard the expression "commit to memory," this is likely what was being referred to.

This process is not always easy, though. Often, we find ourselves struggling to convert pieces of information into permanent mental fixtures. But, according to a productivity guide from Zapier, we can do many things to help ourselves in this area. They suggest, among other things, utilizing some memory-building exercises to strengthen this process.[14]

---

[14] https://zapier.com/blog/better-memory/

EXPLORING THE MEMORY PALACE MNEMONIC

One such technique described by the company is the "memory palace mnemonic device." This, they say, is "as tried-and-true as it gets."

"Invented by orators in ancient Roman and Greek times, the memory palace (or mind palace or 'method of loci') technique is both effective and enjoyable to use, whether you're trying to remember a speech you have to give, details of a case you're working on (a la Sherlock Holmes), or your grocery list," reads the strategy guide.

To use this technique, you must associate a familiar location, such as your home or the route you take to work, with the particular item you are trying to retain. This works because you are "visually pegging" representations of what you are trying to retain with a location that you *already* have a strong memory of.

Says Zapier, it works like this:

> *"Mentally walkthrough [your memory] palace noticing distinctive features you can use to store things you want to remember. Each stop on that path is a 'loci' you can peg the idea or object to. For example, your front door might be one loci, the table in your foyer a second loci, a lamp in your living room another. Commit those features to memory, so when you think of your palace, the route and objects in it will be imprinted in your mind."*

Next, associate the things you need to remember with the loci located in your chosen palace. If it is a grocery list you are trying to recall, for example, picture milk flooding the door, like a waterfall. Once you get to the foyer, you might envision the table cracking from the weight of the cookies you put on top of it. Now, use your mind's eye to look up. Instead of lightbulbs, you might instead envision yellow, glowing bananas. Now you know what to get: milk, cookies, and bananas.

While this might sound like "bananas" itself, it is actually an extremely effective way to commit information to memory. Actually, sometimes the more absurd the strategy, the better it works when it comes to memory devices.

CHUNKING TECHNIQUE

Another tactic to boost memory is called "chunking." This strategy is used when you want to make large amounts of data easier to remember.

"You probably use it already," says Zapier. "To remember or share a phone number, chances are you chunk the numbers, so they're easier to remember: '888' '555' '0000'-- rather than the more memory-intensive '8 8 8 5 5 5 0 0 0 0.'"

We do this because our shorter-term memory functions are limited to what they can hold at a given time. However, if we group the information, we can "hack the limits of our working memory" to store more information there. Eventually, we can turn these shorter-term bits of storage into longer ones. Thus, the more we can remember upfront, the more we will retain on the back end.

According to information in Zapier, good chunking hinges on grouping bits of data, finding patterns in that data, and then organizing the items. This works because our minds are designed to seek out patterns and make natural connections.

"Our memory system becomes far more efficient, effective—and intelligent—than it could ever be without such refined methods [as chunking] to extract useful structure from raw data," reads information from Zapier.

TRIGGERS - THE ADVANTAGES OF BUILDING LONG-TERM MEMORY

At this stage in your Inner Genius journey, you might be thinking to yourself, Why do I need to commit anything to memory, though, when I could just search anything and everything on the internet?

This is a fair question. Yes, there is indeed an immeasurable amount of information available on the internet. And in fact, we do believe that using that information in the digital age is an integral part of our learning process. But, no, you do not need to remember *every* piece of information that you come across. This is impossible, anyway.

We do suggest, though, trying to commit more and more information to memory. Why? Because what we do with the information we have retained is just as important as having the information in the first place. Our inherent knowledge is an essential part of our problem-solving abilities, our creative ideas, and even our very survival. The more information we have stored, the more content we have to create and craft new ideas. The more ideas we create and craft, the more we can accomplish.

Everything we have stored in our memory banks is a potential building block for something new. The speed at which we can generate new ideas and accomplish new tasks depends on what we already know. All told, it is inefficient to Google the same information repeatedly, and it does a disservice to our brains to not facilitate the connectivity data we have stored. For this reason, we must work to retain as much as we can when exposed to new information. If we do not, we are inhibiting our mental efforts.

PART 9. SUPER-CHARGING INNER GENIUS

So we have done a lot of talking about how we learn, why we learn, how we can use learning and teaching to improve our social, professional, and academic relationships, and look closely at the physical and mental changes that occur as we learn.

Here we are going to parse through what the actual implications of engaging in this supercharged learning regimen are.

- How can we expand our communication skills even further?

- What are the methods to influence others to act without manipulation?

- Are there specific words that I can incorporate in my written and spoken language that will persuade other people to take action?

Learning should have meaning and purpose. Learning is not merely an academic exercise (we know how that sounds, but it isn't). Learning is meant to do things; it is intended to accomplish something. That is a massive part of what we are doing here.

So, let's explore how you can amplify your communication to get attention and get others to take action.

If you're a parent, business person, coach, volunteer, friend, or co-worker, this section is filled with nuances that you can incorporate into meetings, conversations, and written communication that will influence others to come on your journey.

Let's dive in!

GETTING PEOPLE TO TAKE ACTION

HOW DO WE USE OUR INNER GENIUS TO AMPLIFY FOR ACTION?

There are many ways to use what we know for the so-called "powers of good." When we have vast stores of relevant information or have learned great new ways to think, produce, create and manage, we should share them! It is the least we can do, right?

We can do that by using tried-and-true, sound methods that have been around since the beginning of thought: logic. So let's crack that egg now!

PROOF & LOGIC

The ability to influence or persuade is an exercise in both proof and logic.

In this case, influencers must bring together various facts, insights, and values that others share or can be persuaded to accept (proof) and then show that these ideas lead more or less plausibly to a conclusion (logic).

This is especially important for individuals who have worked toward building solid and valuable insights in the first place. But, again, that is you, the learner (or teacher).

Persuasion itself attempts to demonstrate the truth of an assertion or set of claims to shape a logical argument. However, arguments can be valid or invalid. A good argument should be compelling in the sense that it is capable of convincing someone about the truth of a conclusion. However, this depends more on the person's skill in constructing the argument to influence the person who is being persuaded.

In any persuasive dialogue, the rules of interaction are either negotiated by the parties involved or determined by social norms. Ideally, the goal of compelling dialogue is for the listener or reader to arrive jointly at a conclusion by mutually accepted inference. When both people feel like they have participated in the safe arrival at that destination, we can call that a logical victory.

BODY LANGUAGE

There are no shortages of use for effective body language communication. It is relevant in social, professional, and academic settings. It is essential to know how to use it, and it is just crucial to understand how to read it. We use and interpret body language every day. Sometimes those interpretations are so subtle and innocuous we barely notice them. Other times, though, our body language is hugely deliberate and targeted.

Simply put, what happens at the body level influences the mind. What happens with the mind helps mold the body. So how does the body influence the mind?

When you pay attention to how your emotions are embodied in your body language, it helps you tap into your emotional intelligence. These deeper inner resources go beyond words.

In other words: you can be both more authentic and more effective at work and in your relationships. As humans, we can modify our gestures consciously, make voluntary movements, and display unconscious breathing shifts, skin tone changes, and micro-muscle movements.

We use our bodies to convey interest or disinterest, to establish rapport with others, or to stop them in their tracks. We learn cultural norms about appropriate body language from people of any gender, age, and status in our daily lives and can sometimes discover how our habitual presentations can elicit markedly different responses in other parts of the world

We can use other people's body language to help us create rapport with them and persuade them to make a particular decision or take a course of action. If we focus on the other person or group of people, open our peripheral vision, and quieten our internal comments, we will notice the rhythm of their whole body movements, speech, and gestures. If we then match these rhythms with our own bodies, we will find ourselves being included.

This is not the same as deliberate mimicking. The intent is to match the rhythm without attracting conscious attention to it. When we feel engaged by the other person, we can test the level of rapport by doing something discreetly different and noticing whether the other person changes what they are doing in response. If they do, you can lead them into a different rhythm or influence the discussion more easily.

In larger groups, it is essential to observe group dynamics and identify the peer group leaders. These will be the people with others around them, whose movements will be slightly ahead of the others and change first. If we want to influence the whole group, these are the people to match. This can be achieved by establishing rapport with each group leader individually or simultaneously in their visual field. It is possible to change the direction of quite a large gathering by these techniques

PRESENTATION SKILL

Truly excellent influencing skills require a healthy combination of interpersonal, communication, presentation, and assertiveness techniques. It is about adapting and modifying your personal style when you become aware of your effect on other people while still being true to yourself.

Behavior and attitude change are essential, not changing who you are or how you feel and think. Influence is about understanding yourself and the impact you have on others. You could be doing the most brilliant presentation you have ever created. However, if you have not brought your audience with you, the brilliance is wasted.

SOCIAL PROOF

We use to determine what is correct to find out what other people think is right.

*We view behavior as more correct
in a given situation than seeing
others perform it.*

The principle of social proof can stimulate a person's compliance with a request by informing the person that many other individuals (the more, the better, the more "famous", the better) are or have been complying with it.

As with the other "weapons of influence," social proof is a shortcut that usually works well for us: if we conform to the behavior we see around us, we are less likely to make a social faux pas.

When we do not know how to behave, we copy other people. They act as an information source for behaving, and we assume they know what they are doing. Given that we care a great deal about what others think about us, this provides a safe course of action - at the very least, they cannot criticize us for our actions. The tendency for people to "follow suit" trades on the bandwagon fallacy.

COMMITMENT AND CONSISTENCY

These are two words that have a great deal of meaning in the education field. **However, commitment** and **consistency**, which are the lifeblood of so many endeavors, are not negotiable for supercharged learning. If you review all the many theories and strategies we covered in this guide, you will notice that all of them require steadfast practice. Knowing how to learn is one thing, but actually putting that knowledge into action is another entirely. But, telling other people about your commitment will more likely end up with you being consistent in doing what you say you'll do.

This is Inner Genius boosted, souped-up, and turbocharged. So not only can you become skilled in Commitment and consistency, you can influence others to do the same.

People have a desire to look consistent within their words, beliefs, attitudes, and deeds.

This tendency is fed from three sources: good personal consistency is highly valued by society, consistent conduct provides a beneficial approach to daily life and a consistent orientation affords a valuable shortcut through the complexity of modern existence.

By being consistent with earlier decisions, we reduce the need to process all the relevant information in similar situations. Instead, we simply recall the earlier decision and respond consistently to it.

BEING PERSUASIVE: INFLUENCE PROTOCOL

Various stages take place in any persuasive dialogue. These stages can be regarded as 'influence protocol' and include:

1. **Presentation:** Raising awareness of the problem by posing a question, debating an issue, or voicing disagreement.

2. **Opening:** Agreement on rules such as how evidence is presented, how facts will be sourced, how different interpretations will be handled.

3. **Persuasion:** Application of logical principles according to the agreed-upon rules.

4. **Closing:** When termination conditions have been met. For example, a time limitation or the determination of an arbiter

INFLUENCE WORDS – GET ATTENTION, GET ACTION

Much of how you choose to influence others will depend on you, your personal preferences, and the type of person (read: learner) you are trying to influence. No matter what the exact details might be, though, you will need to get the individual's attention (or individuals) you are trying to influence. In fact, you will need to get their attention, *and* you are going to need to retain it.

Persuading, and all learning for that matter, rely on the ability of the influencer to present information in a palatable way for the audience. In other words, information exchange cannot occur if only one party (the influencer) is participating. Likewise, if that person cannot sufficiently create an engaging atmosphere, then no learning or influencing can occur. It is that simple.

So what are some ways we can help make this happen?

Well, let's consider some **powerful words** we can use when trying to keep your audience engaged. Naturally, these words need to be used effectively and put together in the correct order. Still, on their own, but in almost all cases, these words carry inherent value. They are a great starting point for anyone looking to make an influential impact.

AID TO PERSUASION: POWERFUL WORDS

Some words are simply more influential than others! Sprinkle these in your communication and people will naturally take notice, and be more influenced to take action!

COMMUNICATION IN GENERAL

Outrageous	Dazzling	Splendid
Magnificent	Petite	Ample
Fascinating	Eccentric	Glorious
Amazing	Phenomenal	Lively
Tempting	Tremendous	Brilliant
Tranquil	Appealing	Worthwhile
Incredible	Gorgeous	Abundant
Gigantic	Comfortable	Marvelous
Generous	Tantalizing	Exuberant
Memorable	Spectacular	Superb
Vivid	Quaint	Stunning
First-class	Exceptional	Breathtaking
Quintessential	Unquestionable	Dazzle

SALES COMMUNICATION

Free	Personal	Save now
Open at once	Immediate	Improved
Save	Sale	More #1 choice
Time is running out	You Have Won	New
Reserved	Big	Values
Updated	Hurry	Last Chance
Everyone is...	Urgent	You don't want to miss out

PART 10. HOW TO GET STARTED TODAY

Just like anything else, having a handle on the *theory* is an essential first step. But *practicality* is where the bread is made. No matter what type of Inner Genius Profile preference you have, you will need to exercise it regularly. Learning is done in such ways. EVERYTHING is done in such practices.

Sometimes, when we take on new challenges, we find ourselves struggling with adversity, and the urge to roll over and give up is strong. Sometimes it can be tempting to just call it quits and move on. Resist that urge!

In reality, the most tremendous gains we make as human beings come as the result of struggle. The struggle is how muscles are formed. The struggle is how freedoms are won. The struggle is the precursor to success. And the only way to achieve that success is to embrace our struggle day in and day out. We must commit to it.

There are lots of ways we can help ourselves along the way, though. Building a support system is one of those ways. Do not shy away from sharing your struggle with friends and family or even talking with other individuals going through the same experience as you are. Sharing is therapeutic, and it is a vital part of any new journey.

Another thing you could do to help stay motivated as you expand your brainpower is to periodically reward yourself. While you are making progress, take some time to give yourself something to celebrate your victories. Even small wins are worth noting, and the more you grow, the bigger your rewards should be. Eventually, though, you might find that the progress itself will be the reward and you will no longer need to externally seek positive stimulation to get yourself over the metaphorical hump. That day, too, will be one to celebrate!

No matter what you decide to do, remember, we are talking about unlocking genius! It is not going to be easy! In fact, you do not even want it to be easy because if it were, it probably would not be worth undertaking in the first place. It is hard, and that is OK. So do not be discouraged, and forge ahead fervently and with vigor as best you can muster. You will be glad you did!

YOUR FIVE-STEP ACTION PLAN

1 – UNLOCK YOUR BRAIN FUEL

As discussed earlier, to **Unlock your Inner Genius,** the first step is to unlock your Brain Fuel Profile. This is done by determining how we prefer to receive information from the environment (people, computers, environmental noise). Everyone has a preference for receiving information, your unique **Brain Fuel**. This is your lens to the world, your learning lens, your input lens, your information lens.

Let's review: To unlock our Brain Fuel Profile, we must first determine each different type of profile and unlock the core components and elements that make them work. In addition, the Brain Fuel profiles must be aligned with their derivatives and be aspirational, fun, and forward-thinking (related to future skill sets and our future world).

Once you know your Brain Fuel, you can learn quicker, switch gears to receive information given to make sense to you, and, best of all, reduce learning stress. It's pretty stressful for your brain to be in a 'learning state,' taking in information and sorting it out. So, if you can find out your Brain Fuel preference, then all of this becomes way easier.

Luckily, we have created a really great way to help figure out exactly what your brain fuel preference is and how you can manipulate that information. The link below, again, has some really neat tips and tricks for all you aspiring genius learners. So give it a try now and see what you "think."

Once you've completed your profile, ask your team, family, friends, and colleagues to unlock their Inner Genius and see where you all fit as a group. You will not regret it!

www.innergeniusnow.com

2 – UNLOCK YOUR PROCESSING POWER

Let's revisit those critically important four steps that drive so much of what we will do going forward. This four-step approach will help us improve our learning and communication. The "super freeway of learning," comprised of the Processing Powers: **Connect, Detail, Construct, Invent**.

These four **Processing Powers** allow us to take the Brain Fuel we consumed and whip it into something useful. Information that is not appropriately processed does us little good, so we must synthesize that information efficiently.

Again, and you will notice this is a theme in modern education theory, there is more than one way for this processing to occur. And you will also see, again, each of us has different strengths when it comes to deploying our Processing Power.

Like you saw with Brain Fuel, there are two angles: how to unlock your own profile and unlock other people. It's just the same for Processing Power. Firstly, recognize how you can unlock your own Inner Genius by utilizing your Processing Power to its most significant advantage. Then, turn the tables and discover the possibilities when communicating, teaching, coaching, presenting, and talking to other people. It's a little trickier than Brain Fuel Keys, but the Processing Power keys are available to you.

3 - DISCOVER PEOPLE'S INNER GENIUS AROUND YOU

The people around you will be wildly important to you as both a learner and as a teacher. In case you could not tell, supercharged learning is *NOT* an isolated proposition. All of this will be done in the context of social constructs, professional hierarchies, and academic or corporate institutions. We are doing this together.

As we discussed above, there are many ways that you can unlock the Inner Genius of those around you. First, as we discussed, you must identify what their Inner Genius Archetype is. Then you must tap into that profile.

It is because learning is so socialized that we must learn how to tap into the profiles of those around us. When we start to speak the learning language of those around us, the connections we make with them become stronger and more resilient than they would have been before we started supercharging our genius.

The process to discover the genius of those around us is far more than just a means to an academic end, too. It can be enriching from an interpersonal standpoint, and quite honestly, can even be fun. There is a great deal of meaning that can be derived from cultivating these interactions; they can be emotionally fulfilling and academically fulfilling.

4 - THINK ABOUT EVERY COMMUNICATION OPPORTUNITY

The chances to learn, grow and communicate with others are remarkable benefits that we enjoy every day. Unfortunately, these opportunities are too often taken for granted. The most important way to protect against this is to indeed center ourselves and be present in each moment of opportunity. Be aware that every moment is a chance to grow and better ourselves. Every interaction, every lesson, every class, and every person we encounter is a gift; do not waste those precious presents.

Now that you are primed and ready to start supercharging your learning, you will see that there is so much ahead of you. The opportunities are endless, and the only thing that is going to hold you back is you. You have it within you to achieve and unlock so many wonderful things.

We truly hope that now that you have taken in all we have discussed, that you will be able to tap into your inner genius and bring out the best of yourself and the best in others. Be sure you do not let these fantastic opportunities pass you by! They are there for the taking.

5 – REFLECT AND CELEBRATE SUCCESS

This is the fun part. It is also the important part. This whole supercharging business is hard work! It is imperative that as you make gains, you celebrate those successes. You earned that!

Your mental energy is valuable, and when you expend that energy, you must replenish it. One crucial way to do this is by taking the time to rest, reflect and restore. This goes for everything from doing physical work to processing information. Taking care of your body and mind is just as important as cultivating any one particular academic consideration or another. Being a supercharged genius is important, and so is being mentally healthy and happy.

To find the right balance, it is essential to, well, find the right balance. Take steps forward, take steps back. Take steps forward, take steps sideways. All that matters is that you are making progress comfortably and consistently.

There are many ways that you can accomplish this reflection and celebration. They can range from small physical rewards all the way to periods of unfettered rest and relaxation. Find what works for you. Mix in the big and the small. If you give yourself what you need to succeed, you will!

And, always, always make sure to give yourself the credit you deserve for all the progress you made. It will help give you the spark you need to continue, and it will help keep you on track going forward. It is straightforward to sell yourself short and imprint false modestly on your achievements. Humility is a virtue, but so is honestly. If you put in the time and the work, you better believe you earned the right to celebrate it!

PART 11.
CONCLUSION

Learning is a fascinating concept. It is done by all of us, either intentionally or passively, almost at all times in all sorts of ways. It is no surprise that understanding the nuances associated with it is a fairly massive undertaking with lots of different elements to consider. In this guide, we focused heavily on understanding learning from the ground up and then taking what we know about it and applying it in our own super-charged way.

Most importantly, we discussed the biological processes by which information is gathered and stored and considered some ways to leverage that data into the practical strategies we are going to use to make our own learning processes more effective. Understanding *how* we learn is the best place to improve the way we accomplish this. What we now know is that everyone learns a little differently. In order to maximize how we gather and retain information, we must first identify our strengths and weaknesses concerning learning.

Further, we also touched upon the reality that we now live in a world that allows us access to virtually the entire cache of the world's information at the touch of a screen. This is unlike any other period of time in human history and one that affords us great advantages.

Do not waste those advantages!

Ultimately, the availability of information is only the first piece of the educational puzzle. Much success depends upon us to actively go out and seek the information that we want or need and then put that information to use. Luckily, for those who want it—and we know you are since you are here reading this book—it is highly attainable. The trick is to do it regularly, efficiently, and with conviction. This book is here to help you do just that!

As you go forward in your educational journey, be sure to check back in with this book early and often. There is a lot of information in here! You will not be expected to learn it all at once (see what we did there ...). Refer back here when needed, and always remember that the educational journey never ends.

Finally, it is also important to remember that your role in this world is as extensive and magnificent as your newly supercharged brain. You represent the very best of the social and academic experience. You are going to change people's lives. You are going to show people that they are intelligent, special, capable, and unique. YOU are brilliant, extraordinary, talented, and unique.

Every single one of us is a teacher and a learner. We simply cannot be anything less, even if we wanted to. As a civilization, the best chance we have is to acknowledge that reality, tap into our minds and hearts, and work together to bring out the best in one another. The amount that we can achieve together is immeasurable.

Every single day, you have the chance to make this world a better place. You will build amazing businesses, protect our planet, teach our children, fix a problem, and so much more. This is exciting! Do not shy away from this responsibility; you are a part of something unique. As we like to say around here, all that is left to do is to do it!

With that, good luck, learner! You have much to do!

Catherine Mattiske

SEPARATE
ONLINE PROFILE QUIZ & TOOLS
AVAILABLE FOR THIS TITLE.

PLEASE VISIT THE WEBSITE FOR DETAILS:

www.innergeniusnow.com

CPSIA information can be obtained
at www.ICGtesting.com
Printed in the USA
BVHW060231301221
624251BV00010B/124/J